Catalogue of Elymaean Coinage

Ca. 147 B.C. – A.D. 228

P.A. van't Haaff
2007

Copyright © 2007 P.A. van't Haaff

All rights reserved. Written permission must be secured from the publisher to use or reproduce any part of this book, except for brief quotations in critical reviews or articles.

Published by Classical Numismatic Group, Inc.,
Lancaster, Pennsylvania and London, England.

Library of Congress Control Number 2007934508
    ISBN 978-0-9709268-8-3

Printed in the United States of America

Acknowledgements

Above all my thanks go to the CLASSICAL NUMISMATIC GROUP, Inc. for publishing my manuscript, and in particular to my editor, Brad Nelson, the Senior Numismatist at CNG. Brad not only provided most important material from CNG's database but also organized the manuscript professionally, making it a clear and user-friendly numismatic work both for collectors and the trade.

I am grateful to Stephen Album, Jean Elsen & ses Fils s.a., Gorny & Mosch Giessener Münzhandlung, Dr. Busso Peus Nachf. Münzhandlung, Moustafa Faghfoury at Canmoose Coins, and Ancient Coins Canada for their permission to use coin images and information from their auction catalogues and sales lists. Thanks to their cooperation I was able to illustrate many rare or possibly unique coins in this publication. Bob Senior permitted me to use information from ONS Newsletter 155. Thomas Mallon-McCormack, Howard Cole, Patrick Pasmans, and a number of other collectors who generously sent me scans of their Elymaean collections from which I was happy to use several images in this catalogue.

Roland Dauwe, D. Scott VanHorn, Howard Cole, Ed Dobbins, Patrick Pasmans, Dr. Vladimir Nastich, and Dr. Ellen Raven were extremely helpful by providing scarce and difficult to find documentation on Elymaian coinage, for which I am very grateful to them. Thanks are also due to Jan Lingen, who read an early version of the manuscript and suggested important improvements, and Steve Album, who helped me in making the monograph acceptable for publication. Dr. Farhad Assar not only provided essential information on the early coinage of Elymais, but wrote the preface and critiqued the manuscript. His corrections prevented me from making serious mistakes.

And last, but not least, I thank Marieke, my wife, for her help in editing the manuscript and for her stimulus to keep my brain active while writing this monograph/catalogue.

Table of Contents

Preface	iii
Arrangement of the text	v
Abbreviations	vi

Part One. Characteristics of Elymaean Coinage   1

1. Introduction	2
1.1. Geographical situation	2
1.2. Geopolitical history	2
1.3. Language and art influences	3
1.4. Elymaean coinage	3
2. Chronology of rulers and coinage	4
2.1. Early Kamnaskirid dynasty, Parthian viceroy, and the usurpers	4
2.1.1. Chronology	4
2.1.2. Coinage	6
2.1.3. Mints	7
2.2. Later Kamnaskirid dynasty	7
2.2.1. Chronology	7
2.2.2. Coinage and mints	8
2.2.3. Synthesis of mint marks and dated coins	15
2.2.4. Categorisations of Bell, Hansman, and Senior	17
2.3. Elymais Arsacid dynasty	18
2.3.1. Overview of the chronology and coinage	18
2.3.2. Transitional coinage	18
2.3.3. Recent research on the sequence of the rulers	20
2.3.4. Mints	26
2.3.5. Identifier for early Elymays Arsacid drachms	28
3. Divine symbols	29
3.1. Early Kamnaskirid coinage	30
3.2. Later Kamnaskirid coinage	30
3.3. Elymais Arsacid coinage	30
4. Weight standards	32
4.1. Tetradrachms	32
4.2. Drachms and Fractions	32
4.2.1. Early Kamnaskirid dynasty	32
4.2.2. Later Kamnaskirid dynasty	33
4.2.3. Elymais Arsacid dynasty	33
4.3. Sources	33
5. Easy Finder	34

Part Two. Catalogue   45

Early Kamnaskirid dynasty, Parthian viceroy, and the usurpers	
Kamnaskires I Soter	47
Kamnaskires I or II	48
Kamnaskires II Nicephorus	49
Okkonapses	56
Phraates, son of Mithradates I, Arsacid viceroy of Elymais	57
Tigraios	59
Dareios	61

Later Kamnaskirid dynasty
    Kamnaskires III and Anzaze   63
    Kamnaskires IV   68
    Kamnaskires V   74

Elymais Arsacid dynasty
    Uncertain Early Arsacid Kings   83
    Orodes I   92
    Kamnaskires-Orodes   94
    Orodes II   106
    Phraates   117
    Osroes   130
    Orodes III   131
    Orodes IV   140
    Orodes V   143
    Prince A   145
    Prince B   148
    Unidentified king   150

Appendix 1 – Concordances   151

Appendix 2 – Sources, Die Links, Weights, and Size   155

Bibliography   166

Preface

The last major study of the Elymaean coinage was written by J. de Morgan in 1930, *Numismatic de la perse antique*, in E. Babelon, *Tráite des monnaies grecques et romaines*, Vol. 2, Paris (translated into English by D. G. Churchill in 1978, *Ancient Persian Numismatics. Elymais*, New York). De Morgan gathered the then extant material, explored the peculiarities of the various types and denominations, and presented his analysis of the series. In 1986, M. Alram published his *Iranisches Personennamenbuch*. Band IV: *Nomina Propria Iranica in Nvmmis*, Vienna, with a separate chapter on the coinage of Elymais. However, whereas Alram had restricted his general study to the inscribed coinage of Kamnaskires I to Orodes V, de Morgan's analysis involved more or less the entire series.

Ever since de Morgan's and Alram's pioneering efforts, and as a result of both authorised and clandestine excavations, fresh material has continuously come to light, yielding previously unknown types and varieties. In addition, the number of new coins has grown through publication of the material in both private and public cabinets. The increase in both the volume of coins and the changes, minor as well as major, in their attribution to specific rulers has, for some time, called for a renewed study of the whole coinage.

The present work by Anne van't Haaff, a friend and fellow numismatist for many years, offers, for the first time, a coherent analysis of the Elymaean series and lists both material and information from sources that are often inaccessible to collectors and ancient historians. In effect, Anne lays down a basic tool for further research which would serve as a platform for either the refinement of the identification of coinage of individual rulers or development of entirely new hypotheses concerning coin attribution and history of Elymais in general. There will necessarily be further adjustments both by Anne himself and those who have made a life-study of the subject as fresh material is unearthed in the coming years. Nevertheless, in this book Anne undoubtedly offers the collectors of Elymaean coinage and those investigating the history of the satrapy during the 1st century BC – 3rd century AD a unique opportunity to further their investigations by providing the description and illustrations of his personal collection and coins published elsewhere. He begins with a general outline of the sphere of Elymaean influence in south-west Iran, moves to a brief political history of the period based on the Babylonian and other sources, and finally gives a comprehensive catalogue of the series. In particular, Anne's inclusion of the hand-drawings of many coins, all meticulously prepared by him himself, whose details are not always discernible in their photographs, will be of immense assistance to the beginners, as well as experts, and will serve as an important tool in identifying some of the more difficult varieties of the later Elymaean vassals.

I have had the pleasure of reviewing several draft copies of the manuscript of Anne's book and genuinely believe that it is a welcome and timely addition to the slowly growing list of publications on this relatively unknown and poorly presented series. It will not only help us identify our coins but also throw a fresh light on several dark periods of the history of Elymais.

G.R.F. Assar

Arrangement of the text

Information on the coinage of Elymais is not easily accessible as it is scattered among a limited number of old or specialized publications. Numismatists primarily use the publications by G.F. Hill (1930), J. de Morgan (1930), M. Alram (1986), and D. Sear (1982). The first two cover the full range of Elymaian coinage, but are incomplete, outdated, and lack sufficient details for the specialized collector. Alram only covers Elymaian coins with a name inscribed on them. All of these publications are either difficult to obtain or expensive. Further research has been published by G. Le Rider (1965), C. Augé, et al. (1979), R. Vardanian (1986), J. Hansman (1985, 1990), E. Dobbins (1992), and B.R. Bell (2002), but all are difficult to obtain. Le Rider and Augé were important sources of information for this work.

The present book attempts to be a practical guide for collectors and combines available information from the various sources. It contains two parts:

Part One: Characteristics of Elymaean Coinage includes
* The geographical, geopolitical, linquistic, and artistic aspects of the coinage.
* The chronology and dating of the rulers.
* A general description of the coinage of the Elymaean dynasties:
* Divine symbols that are on all Elymaian coins. The analysis, based on research by Hansman (1985), relates the symbols to the deities that were worshipped in Elymais. No earlier catalogue deals with this subject.
* Mints and mintmarks.
* Weight standards.
* An Easy Finder table for every type.

Part Two: Catalogue provides illustrations and type numbering of the coins of Elymais. All coins have a four-part type number, such as: 10.3.1-1. The first digit is the serial number for the particular king. The second digit is the basic type, and is sequential under each king. The third digit is relative to the denomination, and is ordered from largest to smallest within each type. The fourth digit is the variety. In the catalogue, the first two digits are presented together as a heading, such as (using the above example) "Type 10.3." Below this heading is the description of the general type, followed by a list of all the subtypes, by denomination and variety. Using the above example, the subtype would appear as "Subtype 1-1." This is followed by a description of the subtype, with examples illustrated below that are numbered sequentially with small Roman letters. Thus, if your coin is the same as Subtype 1-1 under the heading of Type 10.3, you would list your coin as "Type 10.3.1-1."

The illustrations, which are not to scale, are taken from auction catalogues, literature, and private collections. Many coins of Elymais are small and the details are often unclear. Therefore many of the coin images are supplemented with line drawings. All drawings are composed by the author.

Appendix 1 – Concordances contains a list of the major types and their corresponding attributions in the sources commonly used for Elymaean coins.

Appendix 2 – Sources, Die Links, Weights, and Size list this vital information for the each of the coins illustrated in the catalogue.

Finally, the **Bibliography** refers to the publications that were consulted.

Abbreviations

Album	Stephen Album World Coins. Santa Rosa, CA, USA.
Ars Classica	Ars Classica and Naville & Co. Geneva, Switzerland.
Baldwin's	Baldwin's Auctions, Ltd. London, England.
BMC	Hill, George Francis. *A Catalogue of Greek Coins in the British Museum: Catalogue of the Greek coins of Arabia, Mesopotamia, and Persia.* London, 1922.
CNG	Classical Numismatic Group, Inc. Lancaster, PA, USA.
Elsen	Jean Elsen & ses Fils, s.a. Brussels, Belgium.
Florange & Ciani	Jules Florange & Louis Ciani. Paris, France.
GM	Giessener Münzhandlung, GmbH. Munich, Germany.
G&M	Gorny & Mosch Giessener Münzhandlung, GmbH. Munich, Germany.
Hirsch	Gerhard Hirsch, Nachf. Munich, Germany.
Kovacs	Frank L. Kovacs Ancient Coins & Antiquities. Corte Madiera, CA, USA.
Künker	Fritz Rudolf Künker Münzhandlung. Osnabrück, Germany.
Leu	Bank Leu, A.G. Zurich, Switzerland.
MuM	Münzen und Medaillen, A.G. Basel, Switzerland.
MuMD	Münzen und Medaillen Deutschland, GmbH. Weil am Rhein, Germany.
NFA	Numismatic Fine Arts International, Inc. Los Angeles, CA, USA.
New York Sale	The New York Sale. Baldwin's Auctions, Ltd.; Dmitry Markov Coins & Medals; and M&M Numismatics, Ltd. London, England; New York, NY, USA; and Washington, DC, USA.
ONS	Oriental Numismatic Society.
Peus	Dr. Busso Peus, Nachf. Frankfurt on Main, Germany.
Rauch	Auktionshaus H.D. Rauch GmbH. Vienna, Austria.
RN	Revue Numismatique
SKA	Schweizerische Kreditanstalt. Bern, Switzerland.
UBS	UBS, A.G. Zürich, Switzerland.
Vecchi	Italo Vecchi, Ltd. London, England.

Part One

Characteristics of Elymaean Coinage

1. Introduction

Elymais has a very long history dating back to the Elamites who, as early as 2900 BC, had developed a written language. This introduction summarizes its geopolitical history, its relationship with Parthia and other peoples in the area, linguistic influences, and how its coinage is related to these aspects.

1.1 Geographical situation

Elymais was located between the river Tigris and the Zagros Mountains, an area that presently spans Southeast Iraq and Southwest Iran, and can be divided into two geographical regions. In the west are the flat lands of Susiana, and in the east are the highlands of the southern Zagros Mountains.

In the Hellenistic period, the Parthians lived to the east of Elymais, the Seleucids to the north/west, and Characene was located south of Elymais.

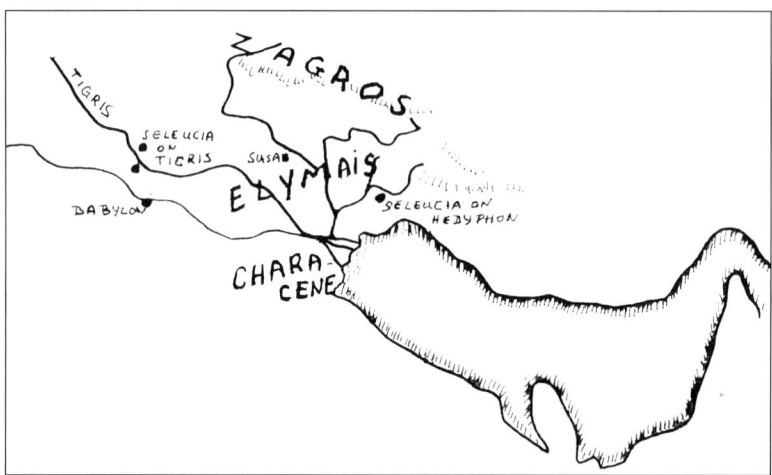

1.2 Geopolitical history

Between 2000 BC and the 7th century BC Elam was one of the most powerful states in the region. Around 646 BC, the Assyrian king Ashurbanipal sacked the capital, Susa, breaking Elam's might. It later became a vassal state of the Achaemenid Persians. Alexander the Great then conquered the Persians and integrated the vassal states into his own empire. After Alexander's demise in 323 BC, the Seleucid kingdom dominated the region. Around 148/7 BC Mithradates I of Parthia captured Media from the Seleucids during a campaign that loosened the Seleucids' hold on the region. This event may have encouraged Kamnaskires Soter to declare Elymais an independent kingdom, and make Susa his capital. The details are as yet unclear, and, in the alternative, Kamnaskires Soter's liberation of Elam may have induced Mithradates I to attack and capture Media. These different interpretations demonstrate that new archaeological findings and cuneiform tablet translations are constantly changing insights to the historical development of the region.

The history of the Elymais and Parthia were intertwined right from the beginning of the Elymaean kingdom. Many aspects of their geopolitical relations are still under discussion. Gradually, parts of the puzzle are solved as a result of ongoing research on rock reliefs, cuneiform tablets, and new interpretations of known documents. Studies by Hansman, Dabrowa, Assar, and several others have integrated these results with information from ancient authors and numismatic data, producing new insights to the geopolitical and cultural history of the Elymaean region. Even more data and insight is forthcoming, as a result of new research of cuneiform tablets relating to the history of the Parthian empire (Assar, 2005). The results of this research will certainly provide new information on Elymais' history.

One should keep in mind, however, that these new insights might not provide a final solution to the many questions on Elymais' culture and history.

The period ca. 147 – ca. 127 BC was a chaotic sequence of wars between Seleucids, Parthians, and Elymaeans, in varying combinations. Control of Susa changed hands several times. During this period Elymaean rulers of the

Early Kamnaskirid dynasty initially reigned in Susa, were removed after some time, and then either set up court elsewhere or returned to Susa. In the intervening periods, the Seleucids, a number of usurpers, and the Arsacids ruled in Elymais. This was followed by an apparent interregnum (ca. 127 - ca. 82 BC), during which time no Elymaean kings issued coins. A new dynasty, the Later Kamnaskirid dynasty (ca. 82 – ca. 55 BC) then set up court, first in Seleucia on the Hedyphon, and later in Susa.

Finally, a third dynasty, the Elymais Arsacid dynasty, ruled from ca. 55 BC until the end of the Elymaean kingdom in AD 228. This dynasty was likely a vassal state of Parthia, and ruled intermittently from Seleucia on the Hedyphon and Susa. In the relations between Elymais and Parthia two aspects stand out. The first is a persistent Elymaean endeavour to maintain as much independence as possible, either as a client state of the Parthians, or as an independant state separate from the Parthians. The second is an increasing Parthian cultural influence, which is reflected in the style of rock reliefs and coinage.

The kingdom of Elymais disappeared when the Sassanians established their reign over the region in the first quarter of the 3rd century AD. According to Hansman (1978), the inscription on a stele of a satrap of the last Parthian king, Artabanus IV, dated AD 215, refers to the eviction of the Elymaeans from Susa at some earlier time. This archaeological evidence, the latest dateable reference to Elymais, supports the hypothesis that Elymais lost control of Susa during the Sasanian conquest.

1.3. Language and art influences

In the flat areas of Susania, the western part of Elymais, opportunities for agriculture, industry, and trade attracted Greek immigrants who had a dominant influence on economic development and culture. From extant documents it is known that in the first decades of the 1st century AD, after more than 150 years of Parthian sovereignty, Susa still had a Greek "polis" type of government and Greek was a dominant language.

In the rugged eastern parts of Elymais, which cover the southwestern parts of the Zagros Mountains, there was no such Greek influence, and the local language and traditions prevailed. The Parthian influence was also limited, as suzerains had more difficulty exerting their power in this region. In the valley of Tang-i-Sarvak, rock reliefs with images and inscriptions of kings and gods have a style distinctly different from comparable monuments in other parts of the Parthian empire. This illustrates a strong local Elymaean art tradition (Dabrowa 1998, p. 421).

1.4. Elymaean coinage

The coinage of Elymais can be separated into 3 groups :

- The Early Kamnaskirid dynasty, with usurpers and an Arsacid viceroy
- The Later Kamnaskirid dynasty
- The Elymais Arsacid dynasty

The Early and Later Kamnaskirid coins have the name of the ruler on the reverse. Some of the coins of the Elymais Arsacid dynasty have the name of the ruler on the obverse (mainly tetradrachms), others on the reverse (mainly drachms).

The dating of the Early Kamnaskirid period types is based on historical evidence of Seleucid predecessors, cuneiform tablets, and, in particular, the Babylonian astronomical diaries that give dated information on geopolitical events involving Elymais, the Seleucids, and Parthia. The dating of the coinage of the Later Kamnaskirid dynasty is based on dates inscribed on a number of coins. Attribution and dating of the Elymais Arsacid coins is based mostly on circumstantial evidence such as interpretation of the style of the images, the type of script, the form of the characters used in the coin legends and last but not least on relationships with the Parthian coinage.

The following sections describe several characteristics of Elymaean coinage that are used for analysis: chronology of rulers and dating, divine symbols, specific mint symbols such as anchor and horse head, letter types and weight standards. These will be discussed for each of the three periods.

2. Chronology of rulers and coinage

2.1. Early Kamnaskirid dynasty, Parthian viceroy, and the usurpers (ca. 148/7–ca. 127 BC)

2.1.1. Chronology
Very little hard information on the early history of Elymaean coinage is available. The coins are not dated and only scattered ancient written documents are extant. New data on the geopolitical situation in Parthia and Elymais was recently discovered in the Babylonian Astronomical Diary registers.

Early Kamnaskirid dynasty
Two rulers named Kamnaskires, one with the epithet Megas Soter and the other with Nikephorus, are identified. Assar and Hansman are of the opinion that, based on numismatic evidence, the two Kamnaskires were one and the same person who grabbed power in Elymais around 147 BC and ruled intermittently until the Parthians captured Elymais around 140 BC. Alram, Le Rider, and Fischer opine that the two Kamnaskires were father and son. While Alram and Le Rider argue that Soter is the father, Fischer argues that Nikephorus is the father, who in 163 BC created his kingdom in the power vacuum after the death of Antiochos IV in 164 BC. For this catalogue, I retain the classification of the two rulers as separate kings, Kamnaskires I Megas Soter and Kamnaskires II Nikephorus.

The chronology and background of these rulers and their Seleucid and Parthian opponents are still debatable. In general, what is apparent is that circa 147 BC two Seleucid kings, Alexander I Balas and Demetrius II Nicator, were fighting for power. The former lost, losing his life as well. Demetrius then went on a campaign against Egypt. The internecine war followed by the departure of forces for the Egyptian campaign loosened Seleucid control over Elymais, creating the opportunity for Kamnaskires I to create an independent Elymaean kingdom. He even campaigned in Babylonia, which he plundered successfully. The response by Demetrius was swift and decisive. In 145/4 BC he ousted Kamnaskires from Susa, and set up his own court in the former Elymaean capital. His residence there was short-lived, as partisans of Alexander I proclaimed his infant son, Antiochus VI Dionysius, the rightful Seleucid ruler. The renewed conflict enabled the Elymaeans to recapture the throne in Susa.

Parthian viceroy and the Usurpers
For the next 10-15 years the Elymaeans maintained their kingdom, although one Parthian viceroy, Phraates, and three usurpers of uncertain origin, Okkonapses, Tigraios, and Dareios, also ruled in Elymais at various times. The question of who ruled in Susa and for how many years during this decade and a half is still debatable. Due to the paucity of hard information any proposed chronology is based on circumstantial evidence and will have to be confirmed by future research. Of the usurpers, Le Rider assumes that Okkonapses reigned shortly before Mithradates I occupied Susa in 139/8 BC, while Assar dates his usurpation to 144/3 BC (see Chronological Summary, below).

According to the chronology first proposed by Allotte de la Fuÿe, Phraates, Arsacid viceroy of Elymais, was the son of the Parthian king Mithradates I. Mithradates conquered Elymais in 140 BC, and placed his son on the throne. Very few coins of Phraates exist, but are critical to his identification. They are similar to the coins of Kamnaskires I and II, except for the legend ΒΑΣΙΛΕΩΣ ΑΡΣΑΚΟΥ. The fact that the legend does not have the epithet ΜΕΓΑΛΟΥ, according to the early authors, indicates that he did not have the supreme sovereignty, but was a ruler subservient to the Parthian king. In any event, in 138/7 BC, Tigraios, apparently a local king, re-conquered Susa, and Phraates fled.

Later authors, such as Sellwood and Assar, do not classify Phraates' coins as Elymaean, but consider them to be inaugural issues of Phraates II of Parthia, struck circa 132 BC. Although in recent years various numismatists have attributed these coins to Parthia, I retain the coins in this catalogue for reasons of continuity, and as an illustration of the fluid political situation in the region. The coin design has the typical characteristics of the early Elymaean coinage and the Seleucid coins struck in Susa. Moreover, the evidence for their placement in the Parthian series is not yet conclusive.

As noted above, the chronology of the period is very uncertain, particularly regarding the usurpers in this period. As usual, most of our information is known from numismatic evidence. The style of the coins of Okkonapses and Tigraios, in addition to the appearance of the monogram on their obverses which are tied to Kamnaskires II Nikephorus, confirm the attribution of these kings to Elymais, and their coins to the mint of Susa. Furthermore, the majority of their coins are known from the finds at Susa (Le Rider 1965).

The recently discovered unique coin of the usurper Dareios (Type 6.1) is most intriguing. The cataloguer of the lot description for this coin in the Peus 368 catalogue placed it sometime before the Parthian conquest under Phraates II in 129 BC. Assar, however, places it much later, circa 127 BC. As this coin is virtually the only evidence we have of this king, any such dating is pure speculation.

Chronological summary

In the period ca. 147 – ca. 127 BC the Elymaeans intermittently controlled Susa. Afterward, from ca. 127 – ca. 80 BC, there is no known coinage from Elymais, and it is likely that the Parthians directly ruled Elymais, and used their own royal coinage as currency there.

The following sequence proposed by Assar (2005) is one of the possibilities for the chronology of the rulers in the period 147 – 127/6 BC (type numbers refer to this catalogue):

147 BC	Kamnaskires creates an independent kingdom and issues his inaugural coinage at Susa, with Zeus-type reverse and the epithet Megas Soter (Type 1.1).
146-145 BC	Kamnaskires issues his regular coinage at Susa, with Apollo-type reverse and without any epithet (Type 1.2).
145-144 BC	Demetrius II captures Susa, forcing Kamnaskires to set up court elsewhere. Lacking the skilled Susa engravers, he issues coins of rough style (Type 1A.1).
144-143 BC	Demetrius II leaves Susa. Okkonapses usurps the throne, and, with the skilled engravers of the Susa mint, strikes tetradrachms of fine style (Type 3.1). [*In contrast to Assar's contention that Okkonapses came to power at this time, other authors opine that either a new Kamnaskires took the throne, or the same Kamnaskires, now with the epithet Nikephorus (Bearer of Victory).*] Assar's opinion is based on the style and high quality of the engraving of the Okkonapses coins. He argues that the engraver of a mint typically is not replaced with the change of the ruler, and placing Okkonapses after Kamnaskires Nikephorus (some of whose dies were very finely engraved, while others were not) would create a discontinuity in the style of the images: *Fine style* Kamnaskires Nikephores → *degraded style* Kamnaskires Nikephores → *fine style* Okkonapses.
143-140 BC	In 143 BC Kamnaskires recaptured Susa, and ousted Okkonapses. The engraver who had cut the fine Okkonapses dies prepared the new coinage of Kamnaskires, now with the epithet Nikephores (Type 2.1.1-2). The contemporary drachms (Type 2.1.2), may not have been minted in Susa.
140-138 BC	Another chaotic period with the Parthians, Seleucids, and Elymaeans fighting each another. The Elymaeans were apparently strong enough to campaign again in Babylonia, creating panic and distress. Parthia proved too strong for them, though. From cuneiform tablets it is known the Parthians invaded Elymais around 140/39 BC, following their conquest of Babylonia in 141 BC. For a period of two years the Parthians were masters in Susa. De Morgan was of the opinion that in these years Phraates, son of Mithradates I, was appointed viceroy in Elymais. Hill, Sellwood, Alram, and Assar (2005) are of the opinion that the Phraates coins belong to the Parthian coinage, not around 138 BC, but later, in 132 BC. [*In contrast to Assar's chronology of the kings, other authors place the reign of Okkonapses during the early part of this period. Le Rider places him on the throne in 139 BC, just prior to the Parthian conquest.*]
138-133 BC	From cuneiform tablets it appears that after 138 BC Parthia was in serious trouble, and a new ruler, Tigraios, took hold of Elymais in 138/7 BC. Allied with their neighbours, the Characeans, the Elymaeans revolted against Parthia, and campaigned in Babylonia, but were ultimately defeated. In 133 BC Parthia regained power in Susiana.
133-127 BC	Parthia ruled directly in Elymais.
127 BC	Parthian king Phraates II killed while fighting the Sacae in the east.
127/6 BC	A new usurper, Dareios, occupied Susa and reigned for a year or so.

For the detailed analysis of the history of this period, I refer to Assar (2005) and Potts (1999). This chronology is generally followed in this catalogue.

2.1.2. Coinage

The tetradrachms and drachms are of silver. The types on the silver coinage are directly influenced by the issues of the previous Seleucid kings. On the obverse is the diademed head of the ruler facing right (see fig. 1). On most of the coins the reverse has an image of a god seated left on an omphalos holding an arrow in his right hand and a bow in his left. The motif is copied from the coins of the previous Seleucid rulers in the region, Demetrius II Nikephorus and Alexander I Balas. Traditionally the god has been identified as Apollo.

Fig. 1 – Obverses on Seleucid and Early Kamnaskirid coins					
Demetrius II Nikephorus	Alexander I Balas	Kamnaskires I Soter	Kamnaskires II Nikephores	Okkonapses	Dareios

Although the Seleucid Apollo type influenced most of the Elymaean silver coins of this period, two exceptional types are influence by other Seleucid reverses. The seated Zeus Nikephorus types served as the prototype of an issue of Kamnaskires I Soter (Type 1.2), and an unusual drachm issue of Kamnaskires II Nikephorus with Artemis/Ishtar (Type 2.2) was influenced by certain Seleucid bronze units. For details on the identification of the gods on these issues, see Section 3.2, below.

All of the coins are undated. Some drachms of Kamnaskires II (Type 2.1.2-1) have the letters HΣ on the reverse that are often thought to indicate a year. It is not a date, however, as this would translate to Seleucid Era 208 (105/4 BC), too late for either Kamnaskires I or II. These letters are therefore simply control marks, and similar monograms are seen on many Seleucid, Bactrian, and Indo-Greek coins. Similarly, the tetradrachms of the Parthian viceroy (Type 4.1) have the letters BA or ΠΤ(?) on the reverse, but these also must be control marks or initials, rather than dates.

In addition to these letters on the drachms, a monogram was added to the obverse of the tetradrachms of Kamnaskires II, Okkonapses, and Tigraios (see Table 1). It is also present on the reverse of one variety of Kamnaskires II's bronze units (Type 2.6). Whether these monograms are indicative of particular mints or simply mint officials' signatures is unknown.

Table 1 – Monograms on Early Kamnaskirid era coinage			
1		Kamnaskires I Soter	Earliest form
2		Kamnaskires II Nikephorus and Okkonapses	
3		Kamnaskires II Nikephorus and Tigraios	
4		Kamnaskires II Nikephorus	
5		Phraates, Parthian viceroy	

Le Rider identified monogram 1 as the earliest on Kamnaskires' coinage, as it is identical with a monogram on certain bronze coins of Alexander I Balas. Three further forms have been identified. Le Rider thought monogram 4 was struck on the tetradrachms of Okkonapses and Tigraios, indicating it is was the latest. For Le Rider this was proof that these three kings ruled in Susa in sequence (but see Assar 2005).

The copper denominations have the same obverse type as the silver, but several different reverses, similar to the issues of the previous Seleucid rulers at Susa. Le Rider (1965) was the first to suggest that the different reverse types denoted annual issues. Based on Le Rider's conclusions, Assar (2005) constructed a chronology of the Seleucid, Parthian, and Elymaean rulers for the period 150/49 – 122/1 BC. Monogram 3 occurs on one type of bronze unit of Kamnaskires II (Type 2.6). This same monogram is present on a series of bronzes of the Seleucid king Demetrius I that was struck in Susa (Le Rider 1965, p. 75).

2.1.3. Mints

Two symbols, a **horse head** and an **anchor,** are clues for the mint places and the chronology of Elymaean coinage (see Section 2.2.2, below). The use of these two symbols is not an Elymaean innovation, but was copied from their Seleucid predecessors, who used them on certain coins for several generations.

The silver coins of the Early Kamnaskirid rulers have no mintmarks. However, certain bronze issues feature a horse head or anchor as a reverse type that some numismatists have concluded are indications of particular mints (see fig. 2). Le Rider and Hansman link the **horse head** to the **Susa** mint and the **anchor** to the mint in **Seleucia on the Hedyphon**. Accepting this link, the conclusion would imply that when Kamnaskires II lost control over Susa he continued to mint in Seleucia on the Hedyphon.

Fig. 2 – Reverse types possibly indicating mints	
Kamnaskires II	Kamnaskires II
Æ Unit (Type 2.3)	Æ Unit (Type 2.4)
Ruling in Susa	Ruling in Seleucia on the Hedyphon

2.2. Later Kamnaskirid dynasty (ca. 82/1–33/2 BC)

2.2.1. Chronology

After the loss of Susa to the Parthians in 127 BC, there is a gap in the coinage of Elymais for about half a century, while Parthian coinage was used in the region. From circa 80 BC Elymaean kings issued coins again, first at Seleucia on the Hedyphon, later at Susa. From the numismatic evidence, this dynasty ended ca. 33/2 BC. As with the previous dynasty, the coinage is the majority of the direct evidence we have available to us today, supplemented by the references to Elymais in the historical record of related kingdoms, such as the Parthians.

All the rulers of the Later Kamnaskirid dynasty have the name Kamnaskires. It has been suggested that Kamnaskires is not a personal name but the name of the dynasty or an honorific use of the name of the founder of the Elymaean kingdom, similar to the use of ΑΡΣΑΚΟΥ on Parthian coinage. However, the legend on Types 8.1-8.3 reads "King Kamnaskires grandson of King Kamnaskires," which strongly suggests that Kamnaskires was a personal name.

The identification of this dynasty's kings is still debatable, and is directly tied to the numismatic evidence. The first Kamnaskires minted coins with a jugate portrait of himself with his queen, Anzaze. This ruler has traditionally been called Kamnaskires III. Hansman opined that the date (ΑΛΣ = S231 = 82/1 BC) found on his coins might commemorate the year in which Elymais regained a relative degree of independence from Parthia, but was still minting in Seleucia on the Hedyphon (anchor mintmark, see Section 2.2.2, below).

The number and designation of the remainder of the kings of this dynasty vary considerably in the references (see Section 2.2.4 for a detailed discussion):

De Morgan:	Kamnaskires II, III, IV, V, VI, A, B, C, D.
Hill (BMC):	Kamnaskires II, III "and successors."
Sear:	Kamnaskires II, III, V, VI (no Kamnaskires IV listed).
Alram:	Kamnaskires III, IV, V, NB1, NB2, NB3.
Bell:	Kamnaskires III and IV.
Hansman:	Kamnaskires II, III, IV, V.
Senior:	Possibly only one ruler named Kamnaskires.

This catalogue distinguishes three rulers in the Later Kamnaskirid dynasty:
1. **Kamnaskires III & Anzaze**. Obverse with jugate portrait; reverse with Belos (Zeus) seated. Dated coins: S231 – S239 (82/1 – 74/3 BC).
2. **Kamnaskires IV**. Obverse with young or older bust; reverse with Belos (Zeus) seated. Dated coins: S250 – S259 (63/2 – 54/3 BC).
3. **Kamnaskires V**. Obverse with bust with rather long beard; reverse with small bust. Dated coins: S259 – S280 (54/3 – 33/2 BC).

2.2.2. Coinage and mints

This dynasty minted only silver or billon tetradrachms, drachms, hemidrachms, obols, and hemiobols. No bronze issues have been found. Bronze coins attributed to this dynasty by previous authors are attributed here to the subsequent Elymais Arsacid dynasty (Type 10).

Kamnaskires III & Anzaze AR Tetradrachm	Kamnaskires IV (young portrait) AR Tetradrachm	Kamnaskires IV (old portrait) AR Tetradrachm

The coins of the first two kings are influenced by both Parthian and Seleucid designs. Their obverses reflect Parthian types. On the coins of Kamnaskires III & Anzaze, the king has a left facing bust with a Persian style hair dress, prominent beard, and moustache. Kamnakires IV's early coinage features a beardless, youthful bust that gradually changes to an older, bearded bust on his later issues. The reverses of these early coins, reflecting Seleucid types, have a bearded god seated left, holding a sceptre in his left hand and Nike, who holds a diadem, in his right hand. Most numismatists identify the god as Zeus. Hill (BMC) and Hansman (1985), more persuasively, identify the god as probably Belos, or Bel, the Elymaean sky god (see Section 3, below). A four-line legend surrounds the seated figure.

Kamnaskires V AR Tetradrachm, early style	Kamnaskires V AR Tetradrachm, late style

On the issues of the next king, Kamnaskires V, the reverse type was radically changed to a small, left facing bearded bust, similar to the contemporary issues of Persis. It has been suggested, as at Persis, that the image on the reverse is the father of the ruler. It may also represent the sky god Belos. During this reign, the silver content of the coinage gradually dropped, and their designs, in particular the reverse, became less fine or even crude.

Exceptional legends
A special feature on some Kamnaskires III & Anzaze tetradrachms (Types 7.1.1-1, 2, 4 and 5) is an additional legend in tiny letters in the inner left field, under the arm of Belos. Petrowicz first published this legend, reading, ΓΑΚΕΔΩΝ. Later, Allotte de la Füye (1902), reported other examples, but read them as ΕΛΕΚΕΔΩΝ, ΣΑΚΕΔΩΝ, and even ΝΙΚΕΦΟΡΟΥ. Alram, however, read the legend as ΜΑΚΕΔΩΝ. All illustrations of these coins, however, either display ΓΑΚΕΔΩΝ, or else the illustrations are too poor to make any conclusions on their reading. Regardless, this legend currently has no explanation.

Dates
Unlike the previous dynasty, the Later Kamnaskirids usually included a Greek-letter date below the legend on the reverse. Unfortunately, these are often struck partially or completely off the flan. Coins with clear and complete dates are rare.

Table 2 – Numerical equivalents of the Greek letters in the dates		
A = 1	I = 10	P = 100
B = 2	K = 20	Σ = 200
Γ = 3	Λ = 30	T = 300
Δ = 4	M = 40	Y = 400
E = 5	N = 50	Φ = 500
ς = 6	Ξ = 60	
Z = 7	O = 70	
H = 8	Π = 80	
Θ = 9	Ϙ = 90	

The direct translation of the dates is not problematic, but there is still debate on which era these dates refer to. Two eras have been used in the references for Elymaean coinage, the Macedonian (or Alexandrian) Era or the Seleucid Era.

The Macedonian Era began after Alexander the Great conquered Babylon in 333/1 BC, and is calculated on the Babylonian calendar. About 20 years later, in 312 BC, Seleucus I, one of Alexander's successors, captured Babylon and started to count his regnal years from that date. This era is traditionally called the Seleucid era.

Most authors use the Seleucid era for dating Elymaean coinage. The argument is that both the Seleucids who we were the previous rulers in the area, and the Parthians, who later became the dominating power, used it. The use of this era creates a gap of about 40 years in the chronology between the last ruler in the Early Kamnaskirid period (Dareios) and the first Later Kamnaskirid ruler, Kamnaskires III. Bell suggests the Macedonian era is preferable, as this would be best in concordance with events in Parthia. **In this monograph the Seleucid era is used.**

Monograms
The drachms of Kamnaskires III and IV generally have a monogram on the reverse. Monograms also occur on an a few other exceptional denominations, including the obverse of a tetradrachm of Kamnaskires III, as well as the reverse on one issue of Kamnaskires V.

The style of the monograms is similar to those on Bactrian and Indo-Greek coins, but only monogram 13 is identical. There is a relation between the date and the monogram type, as can be seen in table 3.

Table 3 – Monograms on Late Kamnaskirid coins					
	**Kamnaskires III & Anzaze**				
6	⟨monogram⟩	4Δ	Monogram on obverse	No Date
6A	⟨monogram⟩	1/2 Δ	Monogram on obverse	No Date
7	⟨monogram⟩	Δ	Monogram on reverse	S234
8	⟨monogram⟩	Δ	Monogram on reverse	S234
9	⟨monogram⟩	Δ	Monogram on reverse	S235
10	⟨monogram⟩	Δ	Monogram on reverse	S235
11	⟨monogram⟩	Δ	Monogram on reverse	S235
12	⟨monogram⟩	Δ	Monogram on reverse	S236
	**Kamnaskires IV**				
13	⟨monogram⟩	4Δ & Δ	Young portrait; monogram on reverse	S250
		Δ	Middle-aged portrait; monogram on reverse	Unc. date
14	⟨monogram⟩	Δ	Middle-aged portrait; monogram on reverse	S251 or S254
15	⟨monogram⟩	Δ	Middle-aged portrait; monogram on reverse	Unc. date
16	⟨monogram⟩	Δ	Older portrait; monogram on reverse	S256 S257 S259
17	⟨monogram⟩	Δ	Older portrait; monogram on reverse	Unc. date
	**Kamnaskires V**				
18	⟨monogram⟩	4Δ	Monogram on reverse	S259 S277
19	⟨monogram⟩	Δ	Monogram on reverse	S271
20	⟨monogram⟩	4Δ	Monogram on reverse	S277

Mint marks
The **horse head** (or, sometimes, a **horse protome**) and **anchor**, which first appeared as reverse types in the Early Kamnaskirid dynasty (see Section 2.1.3 above), are again present on the coins of the Later Kamnaskirids, but now as mint marks. On some coins of Kamnaskires III & Anzaze, as well as Kamnaskires IV, the mintmark is overstruck with a **Nike figure countermark**.

The horse head symbol (Susa)
The horse head symbol has a Hellenistic background and is tied to Bucephalus, the famous horse of Alexander the Great.

As the legend tells us, Alexander was 12 years old when Bucephalus was presented to his father, Philip II. It appeared that no one could handle the great black horse. Alexander, though, carefully observed the horse, and noticed that it was shy of its own shadow. He then ran up to Bucephalus, took it by the halter, and turned the horse towards the sun. Alexander caressed and talked to the horse, calming it, then mounted and galloped away. The courtiers cheered, and Philip was so impressed that he cried for joy and gave the horse to his son. Alexander kept Bucephalus, which became his prized steed during his conquests. The famous horse died 20 years later, from wounds it sustained during the battle of the Hydaspes in 326 BC. Alexander named a city in honor of Bucephalus, which was soon washed away soon by floods–a bad omen!

To emphasize their relationship with Alexander the Great the Seleucids used the image of Bucephalus on many coins. Under the Seleucids, the horse was often shown with two horns, which has led to debate over the identity of the horse among numismatists. Bucephalus had no horns, of course, but golden horns were placed on its head as suitable battle attire for the horse of Alexander the Great. The horse head symbol became closely tied to Susa under the Seleucids, and the Elymaeans thereby adopted the image when they took control of the city.

The horse head image developed over time (see fig. 3). It first appeared as a reverse type on Seleucid coins in the 3rd century BC. Here it was depicted as a realistic horse head with two horns facing right. Then, also as a reverse type under the Early Kamnaskirids in the 2nd century BC, the symbol appeared as a realistic horse head without horns, still facing right. Finally, under the Late Kamnaskirids in the 1st century BC, it appeared as a mintmark, with less realistic features and facing left. During this last period the symbol was also rarely depicted as a horse protome, or forepart.

Fig. 3 – Development of horse head symbol				
Seleucus I AE Unit (Bactria) Horse head right, with horns	Kamnaskires II AE Unit (Susa) Horse head right, without horns	Kamnaskires IV AR Tetradrachm Horse protome left	Kamnaskires IV AR Drachm Horse head left	Kamnaskires IV AR Drachm Horse protome left

The anchor symbol (Seleucia on the Hedyphon)
Seleucus I, one of the successors of Alexander the Great, had adopted the anchor as a personal badge, and its dynastic significance was explained in a legend. As the story goes, Seleucus' mother dreamt that Apollo slept with her and made her pregnant. As proof of his presence, the god left a ring with an anchor device in the bed. Sure enough, she did become pregnant, and the boy that was born had an anchor-shaped birthmark on his thigh. No doubt Seleucus spread the story of his birth to strengthen his image by emulating the legend of the birth of his predecessor, Alexander the Great, which involved a similar divine intervention.

Other (less exciting) theories exist regarding the origin of the symbol in Elymais. One is that the anchor was the symbol of the Elymaean rain god. Another is that Kamnaskires II adopted the anchor to commemorate his conquest of Seleucia on the Hedyphon, a city founded by Seleucus. As the symbol was used only on one type of his bronze units, the argument is not convincing.

As noted earlier, Le Rider and Hansman consider the anchor to be the symbol of the mint in Seleucia on the Hedyphon. Eventually the anchor symbol developed into the general symbol for Elymais. It is interesting to note, says Bell, whenever the anchor symbol appears on Parthian coins there is a close connection with Parthian activities in Elymais.

During the Later Kamnaskirid dynasty the Anchor becomes the most prominent symbol on Elymaean coinage. Except for a few coins that have the horse head and some drachms of Kamnaskires IV that have neither the horse head nor the anchor symbol, the anchor symbol is seen on the obverse of all silver coins of the Later Kamnaskirid dynasty. The form of the anchor symbol originated as a genuine copy of the Seleucid anchor type, but gradually transformed into an inherent Elymaean type.

Kamnaskires III was the first to have the anchor as a standard symbol on his coins. Later, Kamnaskires V added above the anchor first a star or rosette, and later a crescent with a rosette or star. Hansman remarks that the addition of the star and the crescent to the anchor could be a reference to Kamnaskires V's conquest of Susa, where the Parthians had issued coins with the star and crescent.

The development of the anchor type from the Seleucid era to its latest use under the Elymais Arsacid kings is illustrated in table 4.

Table 4 – Anchor/crescent/star types found on Elymaean and associated coinage		
Seleucid kings		
Seleucus I Nicator	⚓	
Early Kamnaskirid Period		
Kamnaskires II (Type 2)	⚓	
Orodes I of Parthia	⚓	

Later Kamnaskirid Dynasty								
Kamnaskires III & Anzaze (Type 7) & Kamnaskires IV (Type 8)								
Kamnaskires V (Type 9)								
Elymais Arsacid Dynasty								
Uncertain Early Arsacid Kings (Type 10) & Orodes I (Type 11)								
Kamnaskires-Orodes (Type 12)	tetradrachm							
Orodes II (Type 13)					Tetradr.	reverse	reverse	reverse
Phraates (Type 14)								
Orodes III (Type 16)	tetradrachm							
Orodes IV & V (Type 17 & 18)	obverse, types 18.1.1-2C & 19.1	reverse, types 18.1.1-2B	reverse, type 21.1					

Nike countermark over anchor mintmark

In the catalogue below are three tetradrachms, one of Kamnaskires III & Anzaze and two of Kamnaskires IV, that have a countermark with a Nike image struck over the anchor mintmark. One of the Kamnaskires IV coins is dated ΑΝΣ or ΔΝΣ (S251 or S254 = 61/58 BC), but the other two coins, unfortunately, have no date. A possible explanation for the countermark is that Kamnaskires IV had it applied to coins currently in circulation to celebrate his recapture of Susa from the Parthians (see Section 2.2.3, below).

Kamnaskires III & Anzaze AR Tetradrachm Undated issue	Kamnaskires IV (young portrait) AR Tetradrachm Undated issue	Kamnaskires IV (adult portrait) AR Tetradrachm Dated S251 or S254

Coins without mintmarks

Among the coins of Kamnaskires IV, all the tetradrachms and most obols observed have a mintmark, except one obol where it was probably struck off the flan (coin 8.1.3-1a). However, quite a few of this king's drachms have no mintmarks. Based on the coins in the catalogue there is an apparent pattern.

The drachms with a young or middle-aged portrait have no mintmark on the obverse (Types 8.1.2 and 8.2.2). Interestingly, they all have monograms 13 or 15 on their reverse.

Most drachms with an old portrait (Types 8.3.2-1 and 2) have the horse head/protome mintmark on the obverse and monogram type 16 on the reverse. While retaining monogram type 16, coins of Type 8.3.2-3 are exceptions, as they have the old portrait but no mintmark.

It is apparent from this pattern that the monograms are probably associated with mint officials at particular mints. Also, the absence of mintmarks on the early coins of Kamnaskires IV, as well as a couple of his later issues, correlates well with the numismatic and historical data extrapolated below (section 2.2.3).

2.2.3. Synthesis of mintmarks and dated coins

Table 5 – Dated coins and mintmarks			
Kamnaskires III & Anzaze			
Date	Denom.	Mintmark	Catalogue #
AΛΣ = S231 = 82/1 BC or ΔΛΣ = S234 = 78/7 BC	4Δ	anchor (early form)	7.1.1-1
AΛΣ = S231 = 82/1 BC	4Δ	anchor (later form)	7.1.1-3
ΓΛΣ = S233 = 80/79 BC	4Δ	anchor	7.1.1-4
ΔΛΣ = S234 = 79/8 BC	Δ	anchor	7.1.2-1
EΛΣ = S235 = 78/7 BC	Δ	anchor	7.1.2-2
ϛΛΣ = S236 = 77/6 BC	Δ	anchor	7.1.2-4
ZΛΣ = S237 = 76/5 BC	4Δ	anchor	7.1.1-5
ΘΛΣ = S239 = 74/3 BC	Δ	no mintmark	7.1.2-5
No date	Obol	anchor	7.1.4-2
No date	Obol	monogram 6	7.1.4-1
Unc. date	4Δ	monogram 6 and anchor overstruck with Nike cmk.	7.1.1-6
Kamnaskires IV			
NΣ = S250 = 63/2 BC	Δ	no mintmark	8.1.2-1
Unc. date (young port.)	Δ	no mintmark	8.1.2-2
Unc. date (young port.)	4Δ	anchor	8.1.1-1
ANΣ = S251 = 62/1 BC or ΔNΣ = S254 = 59/8 BC	4Δ	anchor overstruck with Nike countermark	8.1.1-2
ϛNΣ = S256 = 57/6 BC	Δ	horse head	8.3.2-1
ZNΣ = S257 = 56/5 BC	Δ	horse protome	8.3.2-2
Unc. date (old portrait)	4Δ	horse protome	8.3.1-1
ΘNΣ = S259 = 54/3 BC	Δ	no mintmark	8.3.2-3
Unc. date (old portrait)	Δ	anchor	8.3.2-4
Kamnaskires V			
ΘNΣ = S259 = 54/3 BC	4Δ	anchor with star	9.1.1-1
BΞΣ = S262 = 51/0 BC	Δ	anchor with star	9.1.2-1
EΞΣ = S265 = 48/7 BC	4Δ	anchor with star	9.1.1-2
ϛΞΣ = S266 = 47/6 BC	4Δ	anchor with star	9.1.1-3
ZΞΣ = S267 = 46/5 BC	4Δ	anchor with star	9.1.1-4
	Δ	anchor with star	9.1.2-2
	1/2 Δ	anchor with star	9.1.3-1
AOΣ = S271 = 42/1 BC	Δ	anchor with star	9.1.2-3
ZOΣ = S277 = 36/5 BC	4Δ	anchor with star	9.1.1-5
	Δ	anchor with star	9.1.2-4Λ
	Δ	anchor	9.1.2-4B
ΠΣ = S280 = 33/2 BC	4Δ	anchor with star	9.1.1-6

Based on newly discovered evidence on coin dates Brad Nelson has constructed the following chronology of Kamnaskires III and IV.

As we see from Table 5, the anchor mintmark was present on Kamnaskires III's earliest dated coins, showing that he was in possession of Seleucia on the Hedyphon from that date, S231 (82/1 BC). The anchor mintmark is present on all his subsequent dated issues down to S237 (76/5 BC), indicating that Kamnaskires and his queen,

Anzaze, ruled there both before and after the Elymaean campaign of the Parthians under Orodes I in 77 BC. Nevertheless, the next dated issue, S239 (74/3 BC) has no mintmark, suggesting that Kamnaskires had lost control of Seleucia by that time. Unfortunately, virtually no historical data for this period is known, other than the coinage. It is tempting to surmise that he struck these issues at a traveling court mint, possibly to finance a campaign to retake Elymais from whomever he lost it to, likely the Parthians. What is certain is that Kamnaskires III's reign must have ended shortly thereafter, as no further dated issues, which had comprised practically all of his coinage, are known.

The next dated Elymaean issues appear about ten years later, in S250 (63/2 BC), bearing the portrait of a very young king, as evidenced by the absence of, or only a very slightly evident, beard, a sign of manhood and power. This issue of the new king, Kamnaskires IV, also has no mintmark present, so it is surmised that he was striking at a traveling court mint, and possibly on campaign to reestablish the Kamnaskirid dynasty. His coins have a peculiar legend on the reverse that cites his pedigree to his grandfather, also named Kamnaskires. As the new king's portrait is of a very young man, and the last issues of Kamnaskires III were eleven years prior, and of an obviously old man, it is likely that Kamnaskires IV's legend was referring to Kamnaskires III. Certainly after a decade of his dynasty being removed from the throne, it would be necessary for the young king to promote his lineage to Kamnaskires III, who obviously was a wealthy and powerful ruler, as evidenced by his coinage and relatively long reign. There is, however, no explanation for the 10-year gap between the coinages of the two kings. Were there succession problems for the very young Kamnaskires IV? Also, as his coins mention his grandfather, what happened to his father?

The next dated issues of Kamnasires IV are dated to either S251 or S254 (62/1 or 59/8 BC). This issue, just 1 or 4 years later, shows the king with a more full beard, and presumably has an anchor mintmark that was later overstruck by a Nike countermark (see below). While it is not certain that the anchor was present before countermarking, there was an undated issue before, bearing the young portrait, which definitely has an anchor (type 8.1.1-1). This issue clearly shows that he had taken control of Seleucia at some point. His next dated issues, of S256 and S257 (57/6 and 56/5 BC), bear a horse head or horse protome mintmark, in place of the anchor, showing that Kamnaskires IV had taken control of Susa, and was minting issues there. Further evidence of this event is found the Parthian annual bronze issues of Susa, which Assar has shown ceased to be struck in 58/7 BC.

It may not be coincidental that the issue with the Nike countermark is dated to just prior to these Susa issues. The choice of Nike as the countermark suggests that it was a reference to some "victory." A possible explanation for the countermark is that it was applied to currently circulating issues, not only to celebrate and promote the obviously significant victory, but also to supercede the anchor mintmark as the mint was now moved to Susa.

It is apparent that Kamnaskires IV's occupation of Susa was short-lived; his next dated issue, of S259 (53/2 BC), has no mintmark, and was likely struck at a traveling court mint. As with previous traveling mint issues, these may have been struck while campaigning, and the presence of the anchor on one type (type 8.3.2-4) may indicate that he recaptured Seleucia during this war. If so, Kamnaskires IV might have been mortally injured in the fight, as the earliest dated coin of his successor, Kamnaskires V is from the same year, S259 (53/2BC).

Almost all of Kamnaskires V's coins bear the anchor mintmark of Seleucia on the Hedyphon. While a few have no mintmark (possibly all off the flan), there are no issues with the horse mintmark of Susa. Nevertheless, he apparently enjoyed a long reign, with numerous issues of both tetradrachms and drachms. Dated coins from the period S259 – S277 (53 – 35 BC) are known for this ruler.

There is another question to be answered regarding the anchor symbol and the mint place. Parthian coins of Sellwood type 34 have an anchor symbol behind the bust on their obverse (illustrated to right). Sellwood attributed these coins to Sinatruces, but more recent research by Assar (2000, 2001) has concluded that the issuer is Orodes I, whose reign he dates 80-75 BC. By this time, the anchor symbol had become the royal emblem of Elymais, so the presence of the symbol on this coinage suggests a connection to events involving Parthia and Elymais.  From cuneiform tablets it is known that a Parthian king raided Elymais in 77 BC and expelled Kamnaskires III from Susa. The Parthian king, who must have been Orodes I, may have commemorated his conquest by placing the anchor symbol on his coins. This event, however, is not confirmed by Elymaean numismatic evidence, for, by virtue of the presence of the anchor mintmark, all dated coins of Kamnaskires III were struck in Seleucia on the Hedyphon during Orodes' five-year reign.

2.2.4. Categorisations of Bell, Hansman, and Senior

Bell is of the opinion that only the rulers who issued silver or good billon coins belong to the Later Kamnaskirid dynasty. He is of the opinion that Kamnaskires III and IV is the same person, reducing the number of Kamnaskirid rulers to two: Kamnaskires III, with the image of a god on the reverse, and Kamnaskires IV, with a small bust on the reverse. Bell divides Kamnaskires III's coinage into three periods based on dates he detected on coins.

1. Kamnaskires III alone, bust with youthful portrait.
2. Kamnaskires III with Anzaze, with dated coins: 81 – 72 BC.
3. Kamnaskires III alone, bust with older face with dated coins: 57 and 55 BC

Bell's placement of the coins with a youthful portrait, however, is based on a misreading of the date on the coin 8.1.2-1b. While he erroneously reads the date as KΣ (S220 = 93/2 BC), a die link with coin 8.1.2-1a verifies a reading of NΣ (S250 = 63/2 BC). In sum, Bell's proposed dating for Kamnaskires III, alone and with Anzaze, in his Celator article (May 2002) does not tally with the dates on the coins he reports.

Hansman developed, based on numismatic evidence, a dated chronology of the rulers in Elymais until the end of the Late Kamnaskirid dynasty. His construction is mainly based on the horse head and anchor symbols on the coins (see Section 2.2.2. above). A summary of his arguments is presented below, in which I raise serious doubts of their validity (please note that Hansman's numbering of the Kamnaskirid rulers often differs from the ones used in this catalogue, which are denoted in italics within parentheses when applicable):

- 147-140 BC – Kamnaskires I uses anchor and horse head as the **main** symbols on minor bronze coins from Susa. This indicates control over Seleucia on the Hedyphon and the border area Susiana/southern Media. *This remark of Hansman is not strong: of the 84 bronze units of Kamnaskires, found in Susa and published by Le Rider, only 2 have an anchor and 10 have the horse head on the reverse.*
- 123-91 BC – Mithradates II of Parthia issues fractional bronze coins at Susa with an anchor and a horse head as **main** reverse types, indicating control of the same territory as under Kamnaskires I. *Again the argument is weak: among the 331 Mithradates bronze units found in Susa only 5 coins are of a type with an anchor and no coins with a horse head (Le Rider 1965).*
- 82/1-78/7 BC – Kamnaskires II (*III*), with Anzaze, mints coins in Seleucia on the Hedyphon with an anchor behind the busts on the obverse.
- 77-62 BC – Sinatruces conquers Susiana (77 BC), but after 62 BC his successor loses Seleucia on the Hedyphon to Kamnaskires III (*IV*). *Assar has a different opinion, that Sinatruces was a rebel who never reigned in Seleucia on the Hedyphon; the Parthian king involved was Orodes I who struck drachms with an anchor behind the bust (Sellwood type 34).*
- 65 BC – Kamnaskires III (*IV*) issues drachms and tetradrachms with a horse head (Types 8.3.1-1, 8.3.2-1, and 8.3.3-1 in this catalogue) indicating he was exiled from Seleucia. He may have been the Elymaean king who sent gifts to Pompey in 65 BC, probably asking the latter to intercede with Phraates III, with whom the Romans were then allied.
- 62/1 BC – The young Kamnaskires IV issues drachms and tetradrachms without an obverse symbol. This means they were not minted in Seleucia on the Hedyphon, which he apparently did not control. The tetradrachm, though, was overstruck on the obverse with an anchor, indicating he had retaken Seleucia on the Hedyphon. *No image of the coin is given, so it is not convincing evidence. I have only seen countermarks with a Nike figure.*
- 58/7 BC – Kamnaskires IV issues a silver drachm with a horse protome (Type 8.3.2-2 in this catalogue), indicating he had lost Seleucia and was minting in northern Susiana/southern Media.
- Circa 58-38 BC – Orodes II of Parthia strikes coins with an anchor on the reverse (Sellwood types 47 and 48), indicating he has regained control over Seleucia on the Hedyphon from the Elymaeans.
- 36 BC – Kamnaskires V mints a drachm without an anchor, so not in Seleucia, which is still in the hands of the Parthians. *(This is coin 9.1.2-4Aa in this catalogue. Based on an enlargement of the photo, I am not convinced that there is no anchor behind the bust; the date on the coin is ZOΣ [S 277 = 36/5 BC]).*
- After 2 BC – The end of reign of Phraates IV. No later Parthian coins have an anchor. From now on most Elymaean coins have an anchor, indicating their control of Seleucia on the Hedyphon.

Senior (1998) has published an AR tetradrachm (coin 9.1.1-1a in this catalogue, illustrated below) that is remarkable for a number of reasons. It is of fine silver, the dress of the obverse bust is very similar to that on issues of Kamnaskires-Anzaze, and behind the bust is an anchor with a star above. On the reverse, there is a monogram in front of the bust, the legend is barely degenerate, and the date is read by Senior as ΘΛΣ (S239 =

74/3 BC). This date would place the coin among the issues of Kamnaskires III. Senior suggests that this coin, those of the royal couple, and early Kamnaskires IV coins were contemporaneous and that the different reverses may represent different mints and not different rulers. Over a period of some 30 years both reverses may have been used. The good silver specimens would be the early issues, and the billon coins with less readable legends later issues from the time when the Zeus reverse was phased out.

I have serious doubts on Senior's interpretation of a single king named Kamnaskires. The images on the coins seem to be from two different persons. The coin portraits of Kamnaskires IV has a turned-up nose, whereas the portraits of Kamnaskires V has a straight nose, as on this coin. Moreover, the reading of the date could well be ΘΝΣ (S259 = 54/3 BC), the same date found on the latest dated issue of his predecessor, Kamnaskires IV (Type 8.3.2-3, illustrated below), making the Senior coin the first issue of Kamnaskires V. The fine quality of the coin and the barely degenerated legend comports with this early dating. Senior's suggestion that Kamnaskires IV and V are one and the same person must be incorrect.

Kamnaskires IV No mintmark, dated ΘΝΣ (S 259)	Kamnaskires V ("Senior coin") Anchor mintmark, dated ΘΝΣ(?) (S 259)

2.3. Elymais Arsacid dynasty (Circa 25 BC – AD 228)

2.3.1. Overview of the chronology and coinage
After the Parthians conquered Elymais, members of their royal family were placed upon the throne. This was a common practice for the Parthians, who had done the same in other territories they had conquered, such as Armenia. The Elymais Arsacid dynasty that ruled in Elymais from ca. 25 BC – AD 228 were the result of this practice. Names of rulers and symbols on the coins of this dynasty are similar to those of the Parthian overlords.

Eleven Elymais Arsacid rulers have currently been identified (see below). Although several types have the name of the ruler on the obverse or reverse, there are no dates on the coins, so dating and attribution is based on circumstantial evidence.

Most significantly, the metal for all denominations is bronze; there are no longer any silver or billon coins. There is little evidence for why this occurred, but perhaps the economic situation deteriorated due to a change in trade routes, or the Parthian overlords took the Elymaean precious metal reserves for their own use. A similar development occurred in the neighbouring kingdom of Characene. Persis, another vassal state of the Parthians, however, continued to issue good silver coinage. Either the economic situation in the region of Elymais and Characene was worse than in Persis, or the rulers in the latter country maintained a better political relationship with their Parthian rulers.

The main denomination was the bronze drachm, although some rulers also struck bronze tetradrachms. This suggests that the Elymaean economy was primarily local in nature, and reflects the fact that they no longer were an independent state, but the vassal of another.

2.3.2. Transitional coinage
The earliest Elymais Arsacid coins are clearly transitional types that maintain characteristics of the Late Kamnaskirid dynasty issues, but the obverse busts show a strong Parthian influence. They were probably issued in the period 33/2 BC – early 1st century AD by several rulers who are not individually identified.

De Morgan and Alram arranged these within the (Later) Kamnaskirid dynasty (cf. Alram's Kamnaskirid "Nachfolger" ["successor"] coins - Types 10.1 and 11.1 in this catalogue). Here they are attributed as Uncertain Early Arsacid Kings (Type 10) and Orodes I (Type 11), both of which have many varieties. In general, the obverses have a reasonably well-executed portrait bust. The reverses, however, show a progressive degeneration of a bust within four lines of legend, ending with coins that simply have a jumble of dashes.

While these coins are sometimes confused with issues of Kamnaskires V, there are several significant changes:

1. The metal has changed from billon to bronze (as noted above).
2. On the obverse, above the anchor is, in order of appearance on the coins, a rosette, a rosette within a crescent, and a star or dot within a crescent.

Kamnaskires V Star only	Early Arsacid King Rosette only	Early Arsacid King Rosette in Crescent	Early Arsacid King Star in Crescent	Early Arsacid King Dot in crescent

3. The legend around the bust on the reverse of early issues is composed of degenerated characters, and is unreadable. On later issues, the legend is a series of meaningless characters or just dashes, and the bust is degenerated into a caricature, or is non-existent.

Late Type 9 Kamnaskires V Fine bust, legend degraded	Early Type 10 Early Arsacid King Stylised bust, legend degraded	Later Type 10 Early Arsacid King Rudimentary bust, legend degraded	Late Type 10 Early Arsacid King Crude bust, legend of dashes	Latest Type 10 Early Ars. King Bust and legend now just dashes

It is significant that while the obverses retain relatively decent images, the reverses display a progressive degeneration. This fact proves that the degeneration of the reverse type is intentional, not caused by lack of competence of the engravers. The consistency of coin types in ancient economies was important as a indicator of the reliability of the coinage, so change was often difficult. What this suggests is that the issuers of these coins wanted to change the iconography to break with the previous kings, but they were sensitive to the fact that abruptly changing the iconography would hinder the acceptance of the coinage in local trade. Also, as noted earlier, the Elymaeans were fiercely independent people, and an immediate change from their indigenous coin type would probably have been seen as too heavy-handed.

This desire of the issuers to change the coinage, breaking with the previous dynasty's types, combined with sensitivity to local concerns, strongly indicates that these issuers were from a new, and likely foreign, dynasty. Based on strong stylistic connections, these coins are succeeded by the recently identified Type 11 coins with the name Orodes on the obverse (see below). As this latter type is clearly placed in the Elymais Arsacid dynasty, the former must be as well.

2.3.3. Recent research on the sequence of the rulers

Two numismatists, Vardanian and Bell, have each developed a chronology of rulers that differs considerably from the traditional views of De Morgan, Hill, and Alram. Their suggested relative chronologies are mainly based on stylistic arguments, comparisons with Parthian coinage, and overlap on some important aspects. Although Bell has created an absolute chronology for the rulers, Vardanian has refrained from doing so.

In this work I have made no attempt to date the rulers, but simply mention the range proposed by other authors. Regardless, the relative chronological sequence of the rulers can be determined. In particular, **the sequence proposed by Vardanian, with only slight modification, is convincing and is adopted in this work**. A summary of this dynasty and its coinage is provided in Table 6.

Table 6 – Summary of the Elymais Arsacid coinage			
Name	**Type #**	**Dating (varies by author)**	**Attribution by others**
Uncertain Early Arsacid Kings	Type 10	Late 1st century BC – early 2nd century AD	Vardanian: Kamnaskires BMC: Kamnaskires III Sear: Kamnaskires IV Le Rider: Kamnaskires ? Bell: Orodes I
Orodes I	Type 11	Late 1st – early 2nd centuries AD	Vardanian: Unkn. King Bell: Orodes I Alram: Kamnaskires
Kamnaskires-Orodes	Type 12	Early 2nd century AD	Vardanian: Kamn-Orodes Alram: Kamn-Orodes III BMC: Kamn-Orodes Augé: Kamn-Orodes Sear: Kamn-Orodes III Bell: Kamn-Orodes
Orodes II	Type 13	Varies from 2nd half of 1st century – 1st half of 2nd century AD	Vardanian: Orodes I Alram; Orodes II BMC: Orodes II Augé: Orodes II Sear: Orodes II Bell: Orodes II
Phraates	Type 14	Late 1st century –early 2nd century AD	Vardanian: Phraates Alram: Phraates BMC: Phraates Augé: Phraates Sear: Phraates Bell: Phraates
Osroes	Type 15	1st quarter of 2nd century AD	Alram: Osroes BMC: Choesroes Le Rider Osroes Bell: Osroes I
Orodes III	Type 16	Varies from 1st half of 2nd century – 2nd half of 2nd century AD	Vardanian: Orodes II Alram: Orodes I BMC: Orodes I Augé: Orodes I Sear: Orodes I Bell: Orodes III
Orodes IV	Type 17	Circa 2nd half of 2nd century AD	Alram: Orodes IV / Ulfan BMC: Orodes III Bell: Orodes IV / Ulfan
Orodes V	Type 18	End 2nd – early 3rd centuries AD	Alram Orodes V Bell: Orodes III
Prince A	Type 19	Late 2nd – early 3rd centuries AD	
Prince B	Type 20	3rd century AD	
Unidentified king	Type 21	Uncertain dates	

Vardanian's sequence of rulers
In 1986 the Russian numismatist R.E. Vardanian published an important paper which defends a radical modification in the chronology and dating of the Elymais Arsacid dynasty rulers. His analysis is based on Le Rider (1965) and Augé's reports on the coins found in the excavations in Susa, Bard-è Néchandeh, and Mashis-I Solaiman.

Vardanian developed his new sequence through an analysis of iconographic and metrological data, as well as the relations between Elymais, Parthia, and Characene. His sequence is listed below (*type numbers refer to this catalogue*). **[Please note that his ordinal numbers for his kings Orodes is one less than in this catalogue, as his "Unknown king" is now called Orodes I.]**

Vardanian's sequence of rulers	Traditional sequence
Kamnaskires	Kamnaskires (more than one ruler)
Unknown King (Type 11)	Orodes I (anchor in tiara, Type 13)
Kamnaskires-Orodes	Phraates
Orodes I (vertical line in tiara, Type 13)	Orodes II (vertical line in tiara, Type 16)
Phraates	Kamnaskires-Orodes
Orodes II (anchor in tiara, Type 16)	

Vardanian's argumentation:
1. Changes in the iconographic features of the Elymais Arsacid coinage always occur first on an issue of tetradrachms. These changes are then followed on the drachms, sometimes after a delay. For example:
    a. The Kamnaskires-Orodes tetradrachms follow the tetradrachms of the Unknown King (Type 11), and change the bust from left facing to forward facing.
    b. Early drachms of Orodes I (Type 13.1) follow the new obverse of the tetradrachms of Kamnaskires-Orodes (Type 12) with flat tiara and large hair tufts at sides.
    c. The iconographic change introduced by Orodes I, removal of the hair tufts to left and right of the portrait, occurs first on the Type 13.3.1.
2. The reverse image changes gradually from a bust within 4 lines of barbarized Greek legend into a pattern of dashes. Vardanian suggests that this pattern moves from rather irregular rough dashes to a pattern with fine dashes or points (a "rain" pattern as he calls it) that is an indication of the sequence of the rulers: a rough pattern for the early rulers, the "Unknown King," Kamnaskires-Orodes, and Orodes I (II in this catalog); and a fine ("rain"-type) pattern, sometimes around an anchor or a regular pattern of dashes, in VVV form, little stars, or crescents, for the later rulers, Phraates and Orodes II (III in this catalogue).
3. Vardanian distinguishes two series for Kamnaskires-Orodes, three series for Orodes I (II in this catalog), and three series for Phraates.
4. Like Hansman, Vardanian is of the opinion that the tetradrachms are minted in Seleucia on the Hedyphon. Vardanian also argues that the drachms with the dashed reverse were minted in Seleucia on the Hedyphon as well, and the drachms with pictorial images were minted in Susa.

Table 7 – Legends on coins of Elymais Arsacid rulers		
	Tetradrachms	**Drachms**
Kamnaskires-Orodes	"King Kamnaskires-Orodes **Son of King Orodes**" (Aramaic)	"King Kamnaskires-Orodes" (Aramaic)
Orodes II	"King Orodes" (Aramaic)	"King Orodes **Son of Orodes**" (Aramaic)
Phraates	"King Phraates **Son of King Orodes**" (Aramaic)	"Phraates Basileus" (Greek)
Orodes III	"King Orodes" (Aramaic)	"Orodes Basileus" (Greek)

After Vardanian

5. The legends on the coins are an argument for the new ruler sequence, particularly the expression "Son of Orodes." Three rulers call themselves "Son of Orodes," while one ruler does not refer to his father at all. The traditional theory concluded that the latter king, named Orodes (coin type 16), must be the first as there was no earlier ruler with the name Orodes. There is one now, however, the ruler of newly published Type 11.1 with the name Orodes in front of the bust (the Unknown king of Vardanian). It is interesting to see that Vardanian, who had decided on his revised ruler sequence on the strength of his other arguments, more or less predicted the discovery of this coin type when he writes in his article (page 105) "*There must be another person, a certain king Orodes, father of Kamnaskires-Orodes. As*

there is ["was at that time" (this author)] no information on that king Orodes, the question about Kamnaskires-Orodes' father remains open."

6. The drachms of the early rulers Kamnaskires-Orodes and Orodes I have legends in Aramaic. The later rulers Phraates and Orodes II have legends in Greek. Vardanian explains this by arguing that Kamnaskires-Orodes and Orodes I minted in Seleucia on the Hedyphon, where the Greek tradition was not as strong, rather than Susa.

7. The gradual degeneration of the Greek legends on the reverses of Type 10 and the introduction of the Aramaic legend on the obverse of Type 11 are aspects of a radical break with the Hellenic character of the Elymaean coinage. A parallel development occurred in neighbouring Characene.

    A dual tendency is seen in the Parthian vassal states; on the one side, de-Hellenisation accompanied by the introduction of Parthian cultural iconography in the coinage, and, on the other, the persistent urge for the maximum degree of independence. Kamnaskires-Orodes introduced the Aramaic legend on his drachms around AD 112/3, a period when the Parthian authority over their vassal states was weakened by internal problems as well as conflict with the Romans. Later, on the coinage of Phraates and Orodes II, the Greek legends returned. Although there is no hard evidence for the reasons of this change, it is probably due to the recovered authority of the Parthian rulers over their vassal states. Unlike Elymais, the symbolic value of the Greek cultural inheritance was persistent in Parthia.

    Le Rider (1965), followed by Vardanian, opined that the tetradrachms with the Aramaic letters were struck in Seleucia on the Hedyphon, while the drachms with Greek letters were struck in Susa, where the Hellenic heritage lingered longer. Hansman (1990) generally agreed, but also thought that Aramaic-inscribed coins were occasionally struck in Susa, and drachms with Greek letters in Seleucia.

    A final complication has to do with the language of the legends on the Elymais Arsacid coinage. Le Rider found that the tetradrachms issued in Seleucia on the Hedyphon have legends in proper Aramaic. However, the drachms while the drachms also use Aramaic characters, they are in another language. Several authors have developed theories on which language the drachms used and the reason for this difference. See Hansman (1990), pp. 8ff, for details.

8. On the early types of tetradrachms there is above the anchor a crescent with star, and on the later coins (Phraates Series III and Orodes II) there is a crescent with dot.

9. Drachms with a dash pattern on the reverse were minted in Seleucia on the Hedyphon, while those with pictorial reverses were struck in Susa.

10. Vardanian claims that the coin weights are another argument for his sequence, but this is not his strongest argument (see Section 4.2).

Table 8 illustrates Vardanian's arguments with examples from the coinage.

Table 8 – Sequence of Elymais Arsacid rulers according to Vardanian				
Kamnaskires (Uncertain Early Arsacid Kings) Type 10	The reverse images on these coins (4Δ and Δ) show a progressive deterioration. The example shown here is an early issue with a clear head within 4 lines of barbarized Greek on the reverse. This reverse type, adopted from the Late Kamnaskirid issues, gradually changed into a jumble of dashes on coins of the later Arsacid kings.		4Δ obverse	4Δ reverse
Unknown King (Orodes I) Type 11	This king introduced a change in hairstyle on the obverse bust, and some coins have his name (Orodes) in Aramaic letters in front of the bust. Vardanian had not seen coins with the name, but come to a similar conclusion as Bell: the successor of Type 11 is not the Orodes of Type 13, but Kamnaskires-Orodes of Type 12.		4Δ obverse	4Δ reverse

Kamnaskires-Orodes *Series I* Types 12.1.1-1 (4Δ); 12.2.1-1 and 12.3 (Δ)	Kamnaskires-Orodes must be the successor of the "Unknown king." The new hair dress is retained on the obverse, and the legend on the obverse of the 4Δ is "Kamnaskires-Orodes Son of Orodes," and the Δ reverse reads "King Kamnaskires Orodes." The tiara is flat, and there is no small hair tuft on top of the head. On the 4Δ, the reverse type of the previous king is retained, but degenerates progressively. The Δ have an irregular dash pattern or an image of Belos.	4Δ obverse Δ reverse	4Δ reverse Δ reverse
Kamnaskires-Orodes *Series II* Types 12.1.1-2 and 3	The obverse adds a small hair tuft on top of the head. The reverse is a jumble of dashes that only remotely resembes a bust within four lines of legend.	4Δ obverse	4Δ reverse
Orodes I (Orodes II) *Series I* Type 13.1.1-1	The bust type of the previous king is retained. This is *transitional* type. The reverse the legend reads "King Orodes Son of Orodes."	Δ obverse	Δ reverse
Orodes I (Orodes II) *Series II* Type 13.3	The obverse of the 4Δ has the legend "King Orodes," and a bust wearing a high tiara. The reverse has varying dashes in a somewhat more regular pattern than on Kamnaskires-Orodes' coins.	4Δ obverse	4Δ reverse
Orodes I (Orodes II) *Series III* Types 13.2 and 13.3.2-2	Many obverse varietites. The reverse can have the Sky-God Belos, or a pattern of dashes. Belos type reverses have the legend "King Orodes Son of Orodes."	Δ obverse	Δ reverse
Phraates *Series I* Types 14.1 - 14.5	Δ only. Obverse with facing bust. The reverse has a large number of types with Artemis, diadem, eagle, or a pattern of dashes/crescents in a fairly regular pattern. The Artemis types have a Greek legend.	Δ obverse	Δ reverse
Phraates *Series II* Type 14.7.1-1	The 4Δ have an obverse with a <u>star</u> in the crescent above the anchor, and the Aramaic legend "King Phraates Son of Orodes." The reverse has a "rain" type dash pattern. The Δ have a regular pattern of dashes.	4Δ obverse	4Δ reverse

Phraates *Series III* Types 14.6, 14.7.1-2, 14.7.2, and 14.8	The 4Δ are the same as Series II, but have a <u>dot</u> in the crescent on the obverse. The Δ have several reverse types, as series I (but now with obv. bust left): Artemis with a Greek legend, or dashes/crescents in different regular patterns.	 4Δ obverse	4Δ reverse
Orodes II (**Orodes III**) Type 16	All coins have an anchor on the tiara. The 4Δ a have a <u>dotted</u> crescent above the anchor, a <u>star</u> between the anchor and bust, and an Aramaic legend "King Orodes." The reverse has a fine "rain" pattern, some with anchor in the middle. The Δ have on the reverse a god or goddess with Greek legend, or fine dashes in different configurations, often with an anchor added.	 4Δ obverse	4Δ reverse

Bell's theory on the ruler sequence.
Bell attributes, as does this catalogue, the Types 10 and 11 (in this catalogue) to the Elymais Arsacid dynasty. Bell opines that De Morgan's Kamnaskires C and D (Type 10) coins, as well as Alram's NB types, are in fact coins from the transition period between the Kamnaskires dynasty and the Arsacid dynasty.

Orodes I. Æ Tetradrachm. Type 10.2

Bell opines that the large group of copper tetradrachms which on the obverse have a large left facing bust without tiara (Type 10 in this catalogue) were issued by one or more rulers who were under control of the Parthian overlords. Contrary to the traditional theory on the Elymaean chronology (Hill and De Morgan) Bell states that these coins were not issued by a ruler called Kamnaskires, but by a ruler named Orodes I, a member of the Parthian ruling house. Bell's main arguments are:
- The prominent anchor appears on the reverse of the contemporary drachms of Orodes II of Parthia (Sellwood types 47 and 48). The anchor is the royal symbol of Elymais, and is present on nearly all coins of the Elymais Arsacid dynasty.
- The obverse dies of these transitional coins are finely engraved whereas the reverse is progressively more barbarous, eventually becoming little more than a jumble of dashes. Such a difference in quality between obverse and reverse designs cannot be attributed to a lack of professional skill of the engravers. Bell argues that the Parthians took over Elymais and appointed a vassal king who may have been a son of the Parthian king Orodes II. The new ruler, not wanting to disrupt the monetary situation, gradually erased the reference to the former rulers on the reverse of their coins (Alram 463-466), which accounts for the slow degradation of the reverse design.
- A few coins (e.g. Alram NB 3) show a hair dress similar to the Parthian hair dress of the period.
- A rare variety (Type 11) of these coins have the name Orodes in Aramaic letters front of the bust on the obverse. Bell remarks that the title Malka (= *king*) is missing, which is an indication that the power structure in Elymais was uncertain at that time.

Orodes I name before bust. Type 11 obverse

In my opinion, Bell's arguments with regard to this transitional coinage are convincing. His argumentation for the sequence of the subsequent coinage, however, is difficult to follow, as he gives no illustrations of the coins he is discussing.

In addition to the coins discussed above, Bell also assigns all Type 16 coins to Orodes I, which he places late in this king's reign. All of these coins have the name Orodes, either on the obverse (tetradrachms) or reverse (drachms), and the tiara on the obverse is adorned with an anchor. Bell remarks that the anchor symbol in the tiara, and those on the reverses of the Type 16.3 coins, indicate a link with Orodes II of Parthia, who displayed the anchor on the reverse of a number of his coins (Sellwood types 47 and 48). He also remarks on another connection between the two rulers, the star symbol. Bell notes that on these Elymaean coins, the star has been removed from within the crescent to a more prominent location, as an individual symbol, between the bust and anchor. Similarly, the Sellwood type 48 drachms of Orodes II of Parthia has a prominent star symbol on their obverse. Bell sees this is a strong indication that this Elymaean Orodes may be the same person as the Parthian king Orodes II. This concurs with the opinion of Allotte de la Füye (quoted by Hill, p. clxxxiv).

Like Vardanian, Bell moves Kamnaskires-Orodes forward in the chronology. His argument concerns the obverses of the coins of this ruler, which have a facing bust with large tufts of hair on both sides of the head. A very similar bust is seen on the coins of Sellwood type 35, originally assigned to Dareios of Parthia, but more recently reattributed by Assar (2006) and Shore to Phraates III, circa 70-57 BC. Arguments for an early date for Kamnaskires-Orodes are also found on the reverse of a number of his coins. While most of his coins have reverses with only dashes, typical of later issues, there are some tetradrachms with a degraded head (type 12.1.1-1A in this catalogue) and one drachm with a bust (Hill pl. LIII, 16 and Alram 486). Bell argues that this would place the coins in the early Elymais Arsacid period.

Bell also sees a similar sort of parallel between Elymais and Parthian coinage on the issues of Phraates of Elymais and Phraates IV of Parthia. Elymaean Types 14.2 and 14.3 have an eagle on their reverse, and, most significantly, the eagle on Type 14.3 has a wreath in its beak. Likewise, coins of the contemporary Parthian king Phraates IV (Sellwood types 50-54) show an eagle with a wreath in its beak behind the bust on the obverse.

According to Bell, these congruencies have consequences for the dates and sequence of the Elymais Arsacid rulers. The reign of the Elymaean Orodes of Type 16 would be placed circa 57-39 BC (the period of Orodes II of Parthia), and the Elymaean Phraates would be circa 38-2 BC (the period of Parthian Phraates IV). This dating is more than 100 years earlier than the traditional chronology, and creates a gap in the sequence of the rulers from 2 BC until the AD 80's, or even AD 109, which is the date of the Elymaean Osroes, the next "anchor" in Bell's chronology.

Bell next sees a similarity between the obverse of coins of Osroes I of Parthia (Sellwood type 80) and Osroes of Elymais (Type 15 in this catalogue), although the coins of the Parthian king lack the Elymaean anchor symbol. The attribution of the Type 15 coins has been controversial. Allotte de la Füye (1905) suggested that these coins (Type 15 and Sellwood type 80) are of the same person; a view also followed by Petrowicz and Hill. Augé agrees, noting that the Type 15 coins are of a different, finer fabric than the Elymaean coins of the period and have no typical Elymaean symbols. However, he does not completely discount the possibility of their being an imitative issue of Elymais.

De Morgan, Le Rider, and Alram do not share this opinion, and preferred to assign the Type 16 coins to a distinct king in Elymais. De Morgan placed this king early, before Orodes I. Le Rider assigned the coins to an Elymaean ruler, minting in Susa, who copied the design from the Parthian king Osroes I. Alram lists the king after Kamnaskires-Orodes and before Orodes III. Bell retains the coins in the Elymaean series, but doubts whether there was a separate Elymaean king Osroes.

The reverse of the Elymaean Osroes' Type 15 coinage has Artemis standing, with a legend on one variety (Type 15.1, illustrated to left) read by Petrowicz as ΒΑΙΛΕΥΖ ΧΟΣΡΟΙ. This reverse type is very similar to the reverses of the Elymaean Phraates (Type 14), which argues for a distinct Elymaean king Osroes whose reign immediately followed that of Phraates; much earlier than Bell argues (see Section 3.3, below, for more details on this controversy).

Bell solves the gap between the Elymaean Phraates and Osroes with a two-part argument. First, Kamnaskires-Orodes had two reigns, with his second reign directly after Phraates, from 2 BC – AD 20. Second, the remaining gap of about 80-90 years was filled with "frozen" types and local imitations issued during a period of direct Parthian administration over Elymais. In a private communication, Bell identified the "frozen" types as "crude drachms with dashes on the reverse and illustrated in [Hill] pl. XLI, 17-21." After a close examination of these coins (all of Type 14.7.2-3) I am of the opinion that their engraving is not inferior to those of the corresponding types with Artemis or Fortuna on the reverse. These coins are not "frozen" types issued during a kind of interregnum. Bell's argument for filling the gap is also problematic in that it fails to explain the striking similarity between the reverse types of Phraates' and Osroes' coins, despite the long interval between them in his chronology.

Bell's sequence, although not his dating, of the subsequent rulers, Orodes III, Orodes IV, the two princes, and the "unidentified king" of the closing years of the Arsacid dynasty, is the same as in the traditional chronology.

In sum, I do not agree with Bell's chronology for the Arsacid dynasty, although he has made some strong arguments.

2.3.4. Mints

At the beginning of this dynasty, all coinage was produced at Seleucia on the Hedyphon. Susa only resumed minting Elymaean coinage when the capital shifted from Seleucia, about a century after it last struck coins, under Kamnaskires IV. The assumed date for the move of the Elymaean capital from Seleucia to Susa varies among authors. Le Rider mentions AD 45 as a possibility. Hansman opines that the Elymais Arsacid dynasty began its coinage in Susa in AD 71, based on a coin of early dynastic style with a date he reads as ΤΠΔ (S384 = AD 71). Vardanian, however, mentions the possibility that the move was even later: late 1st century – middle of the 2nd decade of the 2nd century AD.

By the time minting resumed in Susa, the anchor was strictly a royal emblem; no longer a mintmark strictly for Seleucia on the Hedyphon. All copper coins of the Elymais Arsacid dynasty have the anchor on the obverse, and some on the reverse as well. Only the coins of the rulers in the final years of Elymaean independence, Prince A and Prince B, do not have the anchor. Quite possibly these were rulers of a different, final Elymaean dynasty.

During this period the anchor mark underwent a transformation (see Table 4 above). At the beginning of the dynasty, the anchor was always accompanied above by a crescent with a star or rosette. On the coinage of later rulers, the star or rosette evolved into a small cross and, ultimately, a dot.

Most importantly, while the anchor symbol itself was no longer a mintmark, the variations in its crossbars became indicative of the mint.

Cross bars on the anchor as indication of mint
It has been noted that the anchor symbol on coins of the Elymais Arsacid dynasty can have one, two, or three crossbars. Previously, this had been considered an indication of value, but more recent discoveries have revealed that variations in the quantity of crossbars occur on both tetradrachms and drachms.

Dobbins and Hansman published the quantity of Elymais Arsacid coins with **one** or **two** crossbars, based Augé's analysis of 2400 coins from two hoards found at two Elymaean temple sites excavated in the 1960s. The coins he analysed date from the middle of the 1st century AD until the late 2nd century AD; the period when the Elymais Arsacids ruled over both Susa and Seleucia on the Hedyphon.

Hansman opines that the quantity of crossbars at the top of the anchor indicate the mint: **one cross bar** for **Susa** and **two cross bars** for **Seleucia on the Hedyphon**. Two drachms and a few tetradrachms of Kamnaskires-Orodes III have **three** cross bars on the anchor. Hansman suggests that this may indicate yet another mint.

Drachms
If Hansman's hypothesis is correct, 55% of Kamnaskires-Orodes drachms were minted in Seleucia on the Hedyphon. The drachms of Orodes II, Phraates, and Orodes III show a different pattern, with, respectively, 12%, 10%, and 1% of coins minted in Seleucia on the Hedyphon. This comports with Vardanian's theory that early issues of drachms were minted in Seleucia on the Hedyphon and later drachms were struck in Susa. Table 9 illustrates the distribution of crossbars on drachms.

Table 9 – Number of crossbars on Elymais Arsacid dynasty drachms (Augé)					
Ruler (this catalogue)	Obverse	Reverse	Type (this catalogue)	One bar (Susa)	Two bars (Seleucia on the Hedyphon)
Kamnaskires-Orodes	A. Facing, diadem, top bun, lateral bunches	1. Facing radiate bust, Aramaic legend around 2. Aligned dashes/dots	Type 12.2.1-2 Type 12.3.1-2	- 137	8 180
	B. Facing, diadem, no top bun, lateral bunches	1. Facing radiate bust, Aramaic legend around 2. Aligned dashes/dots	Type 12.2.1-1 Type 12.3.1-1	- 49	18 23
			Subtotal	186	229 (55%)
Orodes II	A. Facing bust, plain tiara	1. Facing radiate bust, Aramaic legend. 2. Aligned dashes/dots	Type 13.2 Type 13.3	135 235	1 35
	B. Facing bust, crested tiara	1. Facing radiate bust, Aramaic legend. 2. Aligned dashes/dots	Type 13.2 Type 13.3	1 56	4 20
	C. Facing bust, diadem, top bun, lateral bunches	1. Facing radiate bust, Aramaic leg. around reads "King Orodes son of Orodes" only	Type 13.1	44	4
			Subtotal	471	64 (12%)
Phraates	A. Bust left, tiara, with dotted crescent, occasionally legend left	1. Artemis standing right, Greek legend 2. Crescents 3. Dashes arranged like palms 4. Aligned dashes/dots	Type 14.6 Type 14.7.2-3 Type 14.7.2-2 Type 14.7.2-1	160 12 17 162	- - - 16
	B. Facing bust, tiara, two dotted crescents, usual legend left	1. Artemis standing right, Greek legend 2. Diadem and two dotted crescents 3. Diadem only 4. Eagle facing, four crescents 5. Eagle facing only 6. Eagle right, holding diadem 7. Eagle left, holding diadem	Type 14.1 Type 14.4.1-1A, B Type 14.4.1-1C, 2, 3 Type 14.2.1-4 Type 14.2.1-1, 2, 3, 5 Type 14.3.1-1 Type 14.3.1-2	31 16 10 6 4 2 8	28 - - - - - -
			Subtotal	428	44 (9%)
Orodes III	Bust left, tiara with anchor	1. Bust Artemis right, Greek legend around 2. Bust Belos right no legend 3. Bust Belos left no legend 4. Anchor and aligned dashes 5. Dashes arranged like palms 6. Aligned dashes	Type 16.1 Type 16.2.1-1 Type 16.2.1-2, 3 Type 16.3.2 Type 16.4.2-1A, 2 Type 16.4.2-1B	233 48 166 195 13 121	- - 7 - - -
			Subtotal	776	7 (1%)
			Total	1861	344 (16%)

After Dobbins (1992)

Tetradrachms

Until recently, tetradrachms for this dynasty were quite rare. Today they are relatively common. Most examples show little wear, suggesting they may have been given as presentation pieces rather than placed within normal monetary circulation. The majority (85%) have two crossbars for the mint of Seleucia on the Hedyphon.

Table 10 – Number of crossbars on Elymais Arsacid tetradrachms		
	One cross bar (Susa)	Two crossbars (Seleucia on the Hedyphon)
Kamnaskires-Orodes	-	19
Orodes II	-	41
Phraates	3	2
Orodes III	10	3
Total	**13**	**65**

After Hansman (1990)

Letter types as indication of mint

Le Rider (1965) hypothesised that the legends on the coins, which are seen in either Greek or Aramaic letters, are another indication of the mint. A strong Greek cultural tradition remained in Susa, which was not the case in Seleucia. As such, Le Rider assigns the use of **Greek letters** to Susa, and **Aramaic legends** to Seleucia.

More recent evidence, though, suggests that either both mints were used simultaneously on occasion, or Seleucia occasionally issued 1-crossbar coins. Coins of Orodes II and Phraates predominantly (99% and 90%, repectively) have a 1-crossbar anchor and Greek legends, both suggesting the Susa mint. Also, the known tetradrachms all have Aramaic legends and mostly 2-crossbar anchors, indicating the mint of Seleucia on the Hedyphon. However, while most (88%) coins of Orodes I have a 1-crossbar anchor, suggesting Susa, their legends are in Aramaic, suggesting Seleucia.

In sum, the crossbar and letter type criterion for mint place attribution should be applied with some flexibility to the coinage of Orodes I, Phraates, and Orodes II. As for the few coins of Kamnaskires-Orodes that have three crossbars, there is too little evidence as yet to make any determination.

A note on rarity
The size of the hoards researched by Augé (1979) and the distribution of coin types make them a representative sample of the coins in circulation in that period. Therefore the number of crossbars on the anchor is an interesting indication of the rarity of the Arsacid dynasty coin types.

2.3.8. Identifier for early Elymais Arsacid drachms

At a first glance all Elymais Arsacid drachms look similar. The form and decoration of the tiara, however, can identify the early rulers, and often the type. Unfortunately, the pattern of wear can often make details of the tiaras obscure. Table 11 provides schematic drawings of the different tiaras of each.

Table 11 – Identifier for drachms of Kamnaskires-Orodes, Orodes II, Phraates, & Orodes III					
Kamnaskires-Orodes – All facing, flat tiara or just a diadem					
Type 12.1-12.4 - Many variations in the tiara: small hair knot on top or no such knot					
Orodes II – All facing, vertical line in tiara, sometimes reduced to dot(s)					
Type 13.2	Types 13.2 and 13.3.1	Type 13.3.2			
Phraates – Facing or in profile, one or two dotted crescents in tiara					
Type 14.1 facing bust	Types 14.6, 7, 8 bust in profile	Types 14.2-14.5 facing bust			
Orodes III – All in profile, anchor in tiara					
Types 16.1-16.4					

3. Divine symbols

All Elymaean coins have one or more symbols on the obverse and/or reverse. These symbols seem to have a religious connotation, but their attribution is a complicated issue. The best study devoted to this issue is the article by Hansman (1985), upon which this section is based. While the following presents an overview of his conclusions, the reader is referred to Hansman's article for a detailed discussion.

To attribute the symbols to gods or goddesses we first have to establish the origin of the Elymaeans. Most scholars say they are descended from the Elamites, a people whose history can be traced to the late 3rd millennium BC, and who occupied a large territory that included Susania. An alternative theory, posed by Ghirshman, is that the Elymaeans were Zoroastrians who migrated from eastern Persia to Susiana. Hansman (1985) doubts this connection, based on the fact that Greek and Roman authors never referred to the Elymaean as Persians. Another argument against a Persian origin is the title Kamnaskires, which may derive from the Elamite word *kabniskir* ("treasurer").

A complicating factor in analysing the origin of divine symbols is that over time the symbols became attributes of different deities. Symbols often outlived the memory of what they originally stood for, so new meanings were often created for them. Moreover, symbols and rituals from one cult were frequently "borrowed" and modified by others for their own use, in a process called syncretisation. It is assumed that the early Elymaeans adopted the deities from their culturally-similar neighbors, such as the Sumarians and other Semitic cultures in Mesopotamia. Later, the Elymaeans borrowed from the Greeks and the Romans, syncretising Zeus and Apollo with the main Elymaean god, Bel (or Belos), and Artemis and Athena with Nanaia/Ishtar, the Semitic goddesses of love and war.

The Zoroastrian Parthians used Semitic symbols like the crescent, star, or solar disc, not to honour the Semitic deities, but possibly to convey to the populations in their conquered territories with Semitic cultures (like Susiana) that they ruled through the authority of the local deities.

Table 12 presents the names and symbols of major deities in different religions indicating the syncretisation of the Greek-Elymaean and Semitic-Zoroastrian deities.

Table 12 – Names and symbols of major deities			
Greek	**Elymaean**	**Semitic**	**Zoroastrian**
Zeus Apollo	Bel(os), (cornucopia, eagle, diadem)	Sin - Moon god (crescent)	Ahura Mazda (Fire altar)
		Marduk - Sky god	
Artemis	Artemis/Ishtar/Nanaia (?) (bow, quiver and arrow)	Nanaia/Ishtar - goddes of love/war (star)	Anahita/Ishtar
Athena	Athena/Ishtar (shield and spear)		
		Shamash - Sun god, son of Sin (solar disc)	Mithra

3.1. Early Kamnaskirid coinage
The reverse types of these kings show an image similar to those of the previous Seleucid kings: a seated god holding a sceptre and Nike, or holding a bow and arrow. While these were Zeus and Apollo, respectively, for the Seleucids, on Elymaean coinage the god may be their god of the Sky, Bel/Belos.

Seleucid reverses – Alexander I Balas – Apollo & Zeus	
Early Kamnaskirid reverses – Kamnaskires I Soter – Bel/Belos	

3.2. Late Kamnaskirid coinage
The coins of **Kamnaskires III** and **Kamnaskires IV** retain the Zeus-like reverse type from the early Kamnaskirids. Both Hill (p. clxxxiii) and Hansman (1985) concur that this image represents Bel/Belos.

The coins of **Kamnaskires V** break with the previous iconography, and introduce a number of innovations. The obverse has a star above the anchor symbol. The star is a symbol of Venus, an attribute of Ishtar, the goddess of Love and War. The reverse of this king's coins display a bearded bust. While some authors opine that this head represents the father of Kamnaskires V, others think it is the head of an Elymaean Semitic deity syncretised with Heracles, who was widely worshipped in the region.

3.3. Elymais Arsacid coinage
The rulers of this dynasty used several divine symbols attributed to Bel(os), Artemis/Ishtar, and Athena/Ishtar on their coins.

The coins of the **Uncertain Early Arsacid Kings** (type 10) on the obverse show the crescent with a star (sometimes reduced to a pellet) and often an additional pellet near the anchor. While the star is continued from the previous dynasty, the crescent is new, and considered to represent Sin, the god of the Moon. The pellet represents the Solar Disc, the attribute of Shamash, the Sun god. The reverse of Type 10 coins continue to use the bearded bust from the previous king.

Practically all of the obverses of all kings of this dynasty continued to use the triad of symbols from seen on this king's obverse, crescent with dot and star. Usually, only the star or pellet appear within the crescent, but sometimes the third symbol is added between the bust and the anchor symbol.

Kamnaskires-Orodes and **Orodes II** both issued coins with on the reverse a small facing bust with large hair tufts on both sides of the head and emitting rays (Types 12.2 and 13.3). The early authors have identified this as the deity Artemis-Ishtar. Hansman disagrees and identifies the image as a Sun deity, probably the Semitic Sun god Shamash, again referring to the Rock relief Ana at Tang-I Sarvak.

Phraates issued a number of series with different divine symbols as reverse type. Types 14.1 and 14.6 shows an image of Artemis holding a bow and plucking an arrow from her quiver. This is a well-known representation of Artemis in classical art. The Types 14.2 and 14.3 show an eagle on the reverse. In ancient Greece the eagle was a common symbol of Zeus. On Type 14.3 the eagle holds a diadem with ties in its beak. Hansman interprets this image as the Sky god Bel presenting the diadem of kingship. The third series, Type 14.4, shows a Diadem with one or two ribbons on the reverse, again a reference to Bel. Both the eagle and the diadem are symbols of divine investiture.

Orodes III issued two series with different divine symbols on their reverse. One series displays a turreted female bust that is occasionally radiate (Types 16.1). She is generally identified as a deity syncretised with Artemis, who was worshipped in Elymais. The ancient authors Polybius and Josephus report that in 164 BC the Seleucid king Antiochos IV (175-164 BC) tried to rob the temple of Artemis in Elymais.

Another series (Types 16.2) displays the bust of a clearly male figure with a cornucopia behind. Traditionally the figure was identified as goddess Fortune, who is a female. Hansman (1985), however, refers to the rock relief in Tangi-i Sarvak in which the god Bel is holding a cornucopia and touching the King. Hansman concludes that, by analogy, the reverse image on the coin is of Bel. The cornucopia, as a symbol of the Bel-syncretised Greek and Roman sky gods Zeus and Jupiter, would symbolize the gods' connection with creativity and fruitful abundance.

Prince a uses an Artemis reverse type similar to the reverses on the Types 14.1 and 14.6 of Phraates.

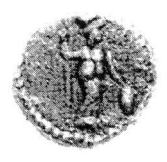

Prince b, the last of the Elymaean rulers, presents on the reverse of his coins an image of Athena-Ishtar with shield and spear. A similar image is visible in the rock relief Ana at Tang-i Sarvak

4. Weight Standards

4.1. Tetradrachms

The weight standard of the Elymaean tetradrachms begins at the standard used under the last Seleucid kings to control Susa, Demetrius I (162-150 BC) and Alexander I Balas (150-145 BC), who lost control of Elymais ca. 147 BC. Afterward, there appears to be a relationship between the weight standards of the Elymaean and Parthian tetradrachms of the period 147-55 BC, as illustrated in table 14.

Table 13 – Average weight and weight ranges of tetradrachms			
	Number of coins	Average weight	Weight range
Seleucid kings			
Demetrius I	32	16.45 gr.	-
Alexander I Balas	16	16.55 gr.	-
Early Kamnaskirid dynasty			
Kamnaskires I and II	12	16.16 gr.	14.92-16.70 gr.
Late Kamnaskirid dynasty			
Kamnaskires III and IV	9	15.49 gr.	13.62-16.08 gr.
Kamnaskires V	7	15.33 gr.	14.48-15.68 gr.
Elymais Arsacid dynasty			
Early Arsacid Kings	38	15.10 gr.	13.73-15.85 gr.
Kamnaskires-Orodes	21	14.75 gr.	13.69-15.33 gr.
Orodes I	15	14.04 gr.	11.30-15.31 gr.
Phraates	7	14.53 gr.	13.16-15.38 gr.
Orodes II	41	15.13 gr.	11.82-16.13 gr.

Table 14 – Average weights and weight ranges of Elymaean & Parthian tetradrachms	
Elymais	**Parthia**
	Mithradates I (171-132) 15.80 gr.; 15.34-16.42 gr. (7 coins)
Kamn. I/II (147-139) 16.16 gr.; 14.92-16.70 gr. (12 coins)	
	Phraates II (138-127) 16.11 gr.; 15.89-16.39 gr. (10 coins)
	Bagases (127-126) 15.88 gr.; 13.39-16.28 gr. (17 coins)
	Mithradates II (123-88) 15.99 gr.; 15.62-16.56 gr. (8 coins)
Kamn. III & IV (90-55) 15.49 gr.; 13.62-16.08 gr. (9 coins)	
Kamn. V (55-35) 15.33 gr.; 14.48-15.68 gr. (7 coins)	

4.2. Drachms and Fractions

4.2.1. Early Kamnaskirid dynasty

Silver Drachms: The extremely rare silver drachms of Kamnaskires I and II weigh approximately 4 grams.

Bronze units and half units: An analysis of the coins documented by Le Rider (1965) provides a picture of the weight structure of the bronze issues in Susa in the period 147 – 133/32 BC as depicted in table 15.

Table 15 – Average weight and weight ranges of Susa mint units and half units			
	Number of coins	Average weight	Weight range
Kamnaskires I and II (147 – 140 BC)			
Units	77	2.25 gr.	1.31 – 3.80 gr.
Half units	1	1.12 gr.	1.12 gr.
Mithradates I of Parthia (140 – 139/8 BC)			
Units	37	2.12 gr.	1.46 – 2.91 gr.
Half units	5	1.30 gr.	1.21 – 1.38 gr.
Phraates II of Parthia (first reign at Susa, 139/8 – 138/7 BC)			
Unit	23	1.96 gr.	1.44 – 2.70 gr.
Half units	2	0.98 gr.	0.91 – 1.05 gr.
Tigraios (138/7 – 133/2 BC)			
Units	69	1.97 gr.	1.28 – 2.78 gr.
Half units	-	-	-

As indicated by the data, the average weight of the bronze coinage at Susa was very consistent over the entire period.

4.2.2. Later Kamnaskirid dynasty

The silver drachms and fractions of this dynasty are relatively rare, and the quantity of coins available for study are too few to show truly representative data, particularly regarding the hemidrachms and obols. In general, the coinage began under Kamnaskires III with high quality silver, and thereafter the quality declined until they were little more than billon under Kamnaskires V. Table 16 shows the available data on drachms.

Table 16 – Average weight and weight ranges of Late Kamnaskirid drachms			
	Number of coins	Average weight	Weight range
Kamnaskires III	6	3.72 gr.	3.45 – 3.94 gr.
Kamnaskires IV	11	3.75 gr.	3.25 – 4.27 gr.
Kamnaskires V	6	3.62 gr.	3.27 – 3.85 gr.

4.2.3. Elymais Arsacid dynasty

Vardanian opined that a gradually decreasing weight is another argument for his ruler sequence. Table 17 shows that his argument is weak for the early kings of this dynasty, as the overall average weights over this period show a remarkably consistency.

Table 17 – Weight distribution of drachms (number of coins in parentheses)									
Weight in grams	Type 10 Kings & Orodes I	Kamnaskires-Orodes		Orodes II			Phraates		Orodes III
		Ser. I	Ser. II	Ser. I	Ser. II	Ser. III	Ser. I	Ser. II	
4.5	2.0 (1)	4.3 (4)	1.0 (4)	6.5 (3)	1.2 (1)	0.7 (3)		1.0 (4)	10.0 (78)
4.0	22.4 (11)	25.8 (24)	31.2 (119)	39.1 (18)	32.9 (26)	25.5 (104)	12.5 (10)	16.0 (61)	44.2 (343)
3.5	71.4 (35)	64.0 (59)	48.3 (181)	43.4 (20)	53.1 (42)	59.7 (243)	58.7 (47)	55.7 (211)	32.5 (252)
3.0	4.0 (2)	6.0 (6)	6.4 (24)	8.6 (4)	12.6 (10)	13.0 (53)	21.3 (17)	22.1 (84)	11.0 (86)
2.5			0.2 (1)	2.0 (1)		0.9 (4)	7.5 (6)	5.0 (19)	2.0 (16)
Total coins	49	93	374	46	79	407	80	379	775
Overall avg. weight	3.61 gr.	3.64 gr.	3.06 gr.	3.78 gr.	3.27 gr.	3.56 gr.	3.38 gr.	3.43 gr.	3.74 gr.

After Vardanian

The coins of the rulers following Orodes III have progressively lower weights.

Table 18 – Average weight and weight ranges of late drachms		
	Average weight	Weight range
Orodes IV	3.1 gr.	2.5 – 3.7 gr.
Orodes V	2.7 gr.	2.1 – 3.2 gr.
Prince A	2.2 gr.	1.3 – 3.1 gr.
Prince B	2.2 gr.	1.4 – 3.1 gr.

Hill, Le Rider and Augé also report units of an "unidentified king" (Type 21) weighing 1.36 – 2.46 grams.

4.3. Sources

Data for the Early and Late Kamnaskirids was obtained primarily from de Morgan, Augé, Sear, various auction catalogues (Classical Numismatic Group, Peus, Gorny & Mosch, and J. Elsen), and the author's collection. Data for the Elymais Arsacids was primarily derived from Augé.

5. Easy Finder

Similar types in the Elymaean series are often found under a number of different rulers, making quick identification difficult. Also complicating the issue is that often details are obscured by poor striking or wear.

To assist in finding your coin in the Catalogue, the following pages present a schematic chart that will identify the **basic** Type. The charts are organized first by metal, then denomination, and then by obverse and reverse type. Some are further divided by major details. Once the appropriate catalogue Type has been identified, the user should consult the Type within the catalogue to determine the specific variety.

It is important to keep in mind:

- The photographs provided are only a generic illustration of the general type, so certain details may differ from the coin you are researching.
- None of the illustrations are to scale. If you are uncertain of the denomination you may have, consult section 4, Weight Standards, above.

Silver (AR) & Billon – Tetradrachms			
Obverse	**Reverse**	**Identifying variations** (if applicable)	**Types**
Head or bust right	Zeus/Belos seated		1.1.1
	Apollo/Belos seated	**Name in legend**	
		ΔΑΡΕΙΟΥ	6.1.1
		ΟΚΚΟΝΑΨΟΥ	3.1.1
		ΑΡΣΑΚΟΥ	4.1.1
		ΤΙΓΡΑΙΟΥ	5.1.1
		ΚΑΜΝΙΣΚΙΡΟΥ (or similar) — **Epithet**: None	1.2.1, 1A.1
		ΝΙΚΗΦΟΡΟΣ	2.1.1
Bust left - double	Zeus/Belos seated		7.1.1
Bust left - single	Zeus/Belos seated	**Obv. portrait type**	
		Young	8.1.1
		Middle aged	8.2.1
		Old	8.3.1
	Head left		9.1.1
	Head right		9.2.1

Silver (AR) & Billon – Drachms			
Obverse	Reverse	Identifying variations (if applicable)	Types
Head right	Apollo/Belos seated		2.1.2
Bust right	Artemis/Ishtar standing		2.2.1
Bust left - double	Zeus/Belos seated		7.1.2
Bust left - single	Zeus/Belos seated	**Obv. portrait type**	
		Young	8.1.2
		Middle aged	8.2.2
		Old	8.3.2
	Head left		9.1.2

Silver (AR) & Billon – Hemidrachms			
Obverse	**Reverse**	**Identifying variations** (if applicable)	**Types**
Bust left - double	Zeus/Belos seated		7.1.3
Bust left - single	Zeus/Belos seated		8.3.3
	Head left		9.1.2

Silver (AR) & Billon – Obols & Hemiobols			
Obverse	**Reverse**	**Identifying variations** (if applicable)	**Types**
Bust left - double	Zeus/Belos seated		7.1.4
Bust left - single	Zeus/Belos seated	**Obv. portrait type**	
		Young	8.1.3
		Middle aged	8.2.3
	Head left		9.1.4 9.1.5

Bronze (Æ) – Tetradrachms

Reverse	Obverse	Identifying variations (if applicable)		Types
Head left - decent style	Bust left	**Obv. symbol**		
		Rosette above anchor		10.1.1
		Rosette-in-crescent above anchor		10.2.1
		Star-in-crescent above anchor		10.3.1-1A
Head left - crude/rudimentary style	Bust left	**Obv. symbol**		
		Star-in-crescent above anchor	**Obv. legend**	
			No	10.3.1-1B-D 11.2.1
			Yes	11.1.1
		Pellet-in-crescent above anchor		10.4.1
Head left - degenerated style	Bust facing			12.1.1-1 12.1.1-2
	Bust left - diadem only			10.3.1-2
	Bust left - with tiara	**Tiara symbol (see Table 11)**		
		Anchor		16.4.1
		Pellet-in-crescent		14.8.1
Dashes - no anchor	Bust facing - diadem only			12.1.1-3
	Bust facing - with tiara			13.3.1
	Bust left			14.7.1

| Dashes - with anchor | Bust left | | 16.3.1 |

Bronze (Æ) – Drachms, Hemidrachms, & Obols			
Reverse	**Obverse**	**Identifying variations** (if applicable)			**Types**
Head left - decent style	Bust left		10.1.2
Head left - crude/rudimentary style	Bust left	**Symbol above anchor on obverse**	
		Star-in-crescent	10.3.2
		Pellet-in-crescent	10.4.2
Artemis standing	Bust facing		14.1.1
	Bust left - diadem only	**Reverse with legend?**	
		Yes	**Features of Artemis**	
			Head left, bow in right hand	15.1.1
			Head right, bow in left hand	15.2.1
		No		19.1.1
	Bust left - with tiara		14.6.1
Athena standing	Bust left		20.1.1 20.1.2

Bust - Artemis, left	Bust facing		17.2.1
	Bust left		18.1.1
Bust - Belos, left	Bust left		16.2.1-2 16.2.1-3 16.2.1-4
Bust - Belos, right	Bust left	**Features of reverse**	
		With legend, no cornucopia	16.1.1
		No legend, with cornucopia	16.2.1-1
Bust - Belos, facing	Bust facing - diadem only	**Legend on reverse (in Aramaic)**	
		King Kamnaskires Orodes	12.2.1
		King Orodes, son of Orodes	13.1.1
	Bust facing - with tiara		13.2.1
Bust - female, left	Bust left		17.1.1
Bust - female, right	Bust left		15.3.1
Bust - male bearded, left	Bust facing		12.4.1

Anchor - in wreath	Bust facing		17.3.1-1
	Bust left		21.1.1
Anchor - in crossed cornucopias	Bust facing		17.3.1-2
Anchor - with dashes or symbols	Bust left		16.3.2
Diadem	Bust facing		14.4.1
Eagle standing	Bust facing	**Eagle with diadem in beak?**	
		No	14.2.1
		Yes	14.3.1
Crescents	Bust facing		14.5.1
	Bust left		14.7.2-3
	Bust right		21.2.1

Dashes - parallel linear pattern	Bust facing - diadem only		12.3.1
	Bust facing - with tiara		13.3.2
	Bust left	**Tiara symbol (see Table 11)**	
		Pellet-in-crescent	14.7.2-1
		Anchor	16.4.2-1A
Dashes - V-shaped patterns	Bust left	**Tiara symbol (see Table 11)**	
		Pellet-in-crescent	14.7.2-2
		Anchor	16.4.2-1B
Dashes - irregular pattern	Bust facing - diadem only		12.3.1
	Bust facing - with tiara		13.3.2
	Bust left	**Tiara symbol (see Table 11)**	
		Pellet-in-crescent	14.7.2-1
		Anchor	16.4.2-2

Bronze (Æ) – Units & 1/2 Units				
Obverse	**Reverse**	**Identifying variations** (if applicable)	**Types**
Head right - diademed only	Anchor	None	2.4.1
	Artemis/Ishtar standing	None	5.2.1
	Boar's head	None	5.4.1
	Bow and quiver	None	2.8.1
	Bull's head facing (no photo)	None	4.4.1
	Cornucopia	None	2.6.1
	Goddess standing	None	4.3.1, 4.3.2
	Hermes standing (no photo)	None	4.5.1
	Horse head	**Name on reverse**	
		ΑΡΣΑΚΟΥ	4.2.1
		ΚΑΜΝΙΣΚΙΡΟΥ (or similar)	2.3.1
	Nike standing	None	2.11.1
Obverse	**Reverse**	**Identifying variations** (if applicable)	**Types**

	Thunderbolt	None	5.3.1
	Tripod	None	2.5.1
Head right - radiate	Apollo/Belos standing	None	3.2.1
Head right - helmeted	Bow and quiver	None	2.9.1
	Eagle	None	5.5.1
	Herm	None	5.6.1
	Tyche seated	None	2.10.1
Head right - elephant skin headdress	Palm frond	None	5.7.1
Head facing - helmeted	Eagle	None	2.7.1

Part Two

Catalogue

Early Kamnaskirid Dynasty, Parthian Viceroy, and the Usurpers

KAMNASKIRES I SOTER
(ca. 147-139 B.C.)

Type 1.1
Obv: Diademed, youthful male head facing right; reel and pellet border; no monogram.
Rev: ΒΑΣΙΛΕΩΣ ΜΕΓΑΛΟΥ ΚΑΜΝΙΣΚΙΡΟΥ ΣΩΤΗΡΟΣ, old, bearded god (Belos or Zeus) seated left on throne, holding a globe in his outstretched right hand and a sceptre in his left hand; no border.
Notes: This is considered the inaugural issue of Kamnaskires I with the extra honorific epithets ΜΕΓΑΛΟΥ and ΣΩΤΗΡΟΣ.

AR Tetradrachms

Subtype 1-1   No variation.

a.

Type 1.2
Obv: Diademed, youthful male head facing right; reel and pellet border; no monogram.
Rev: ΒΑΣΙΛΕΩΣ ΚΑΜΝΙΣΚΙΡΟΥ, youthful god (Belos or Apollo) seated left on an omphalos, holding an arrow in his outstretched right hand and a bow in his left hand; no border.
Notes: This second type no longer carries the honorific epithets and follows the style of the preceding coinage of the Seleucid king Alexander I Balas. According to Le Rider, the Susa mint did not use the extra honorific epithets in the legends of regal issues.

AR Tetradrachms

Subtype 1-1   No variation.

a.

KAMNASKIRES I OR II
(ca. 147-139 B.C.)

Type 1A.1
Obv: Diademed, youthful male head facing right; reel and pellet border; no monogram.
Rev: ΒΑΣΙΛΕΩΣ ΚΑΜΝΙΣΚΙΡΟΥ, youthful god (Belos or Apollo) seated left on an omphalos, holding an arrow in his outstretched right hand and a bow in his left hand; pellet border.
Notes: A less refined issue. While the obverse, without monogram, is characteristic of Kamnaskires I, the reverse, with pelleted border, is indicative of Kamnaskires II. Assar (2005) identifies the coin as a third type of Kamnaskires (I) Soter, which may have been minted at an unknown location during the time Kamnaskires I was removed from Susa by the Seleucid king Demetrius II. On the other hand, this coin may be an early issue of Kamnaskires II, prior to the addition of the obverse monogram to his tetradrachms. One complication is that the epithet ΝΙΚΕΦΟΡΟΥ may be present in the exergue, but the strike is such that it would off the flan.

AR Tetradrachms

Subtype 1-1   No variation.

a.

KAMNASKIRES II NIKEPHORUS
(ca. 147-139 B.C.)

Type 2.1
Obv: Diademed, youthful male head facing right; monogram behind; reel and pellet border.
Rev: ΒΑΣΙΛΕΩΣ ΚΑΜΝΙΣΚΙΡΟΥ ΝΙΚΗΦΟΡΟΥ, youthful god (Belos or Apollo) seated left on an omphalos, holding an arrow in his outstretched right hand and a bow in his left hand; pellet border.

AR Tetradrachms

Subtype 1-1   **Obv:** monogram 1 behind head.
Le Rider identified the monogram on this type as the earliest on Kamnaskires' coinage, as it is identical with a monogram on certain bronze coins of Alexander I Balas.

a.

b.

Subtype 1-2   **Obv:** monogram 2.

a.

b.

KAMNASKIRES II NIKEPHORUS

Subtype 1-3 **Obv:** monogram 2.
Rev: legend variant with KAIMNICKIPOY.

a.

Subtype 1-4 **Obv:** monogram 3.

a.

Subtype 1-5 **Obv:** monogram 4.

a.

Subtype 1-6 **Obv:** uncertain monogram.

a.

Subtype 1-7 **Obv:** rough style, uncertain monogram.
Rev: degraded legend

a.

KAMNASKIRES II NIKEPHORUS

Subtype 1-8 **Obv:** no monogram.
Rev: legend variant with ΚΑΜΑΣΚΕΙΡΟΥ.

a.

Note: As this type has no monogram, it may have been struck while Kamnaskires was not in control of Susa.

AR Drachms

Subtype 2-1 **Obv:** no monogram.
Rev: legend ΒΑΣΙΛΕΩΣ ΚΑΜΝΑΣΚΙΡΟΥ, ΗΣ in exergue, no border.

a.

Note: As this type has no monogram, it may have been struck while Kamnaskires was not in control of Susa.

b.

Subtype 2-2 **Obv:** monogram 2.
Rev: uncertain monogram and Σ in exergue.

a.

Note: The style of this subtype is similar to Type 1.2 or 1.6.

Subtype 2-3 **Obv:** degraded style, monogram 2.
Rev: degraded style, uncertain monogram in exergue.

a.

Subtype 2-4 **Obv:** degraded style, monogram 2.
Rev: degraded style, legend variant with ΚΑΜΝΑΣΚΙΡΟΥ, uncertain monogram or letters in exergue.

a.

Note on Subtypes 2-3 and 2-4: Le Rider remarks that these drachms, with their degraded style, may have been issued in a hurry, either shortly before Kamnaskires lost Susa to Mithradates I of Parthia, or in a short interval when Kamnaskires recaptured Susa during the conflict between Mithradates I and the Seleucid king Demetrius II. It is also possible that Kamnaskires issued these drachms at Seleucia on the Hedyphon, after his expulsion from Susa. Regarding the monogram or letters in the exergue, Le Rider (1956, p. 360) thought this may represent a contraction of the title Nikephores

Type 2.2
Obv: Diademed and draped, youthful male bust facing right; pellet border.
Rev: ΒΑΣΙΛΕΩΣ ΜΕΓΑΛΟΥ ΚΑΜΙΣΚΕΙΡΟΥ ΝΙΚΗΦΟΡΟΥ, Artemis/Ishtar standing left; control mark(s) to upper left.
Note: This type, represented by a unique drachm, is unparalleled in the Elymaean series, and could be imitating the reverse type on certain Seleucid bronzes.

AR Drachms

Subtype 1-1 **Rev:** control mark as ΙΠ(?). Only a single coin known.

a.

Type 2.3
Obv: Diademed, youthful male head facing right.
Rev: ΚΑΜΝΙΣΚΙΡΟΥ, horse head facing right.

Æ Units

Subtype 1-1 No variation.

a.

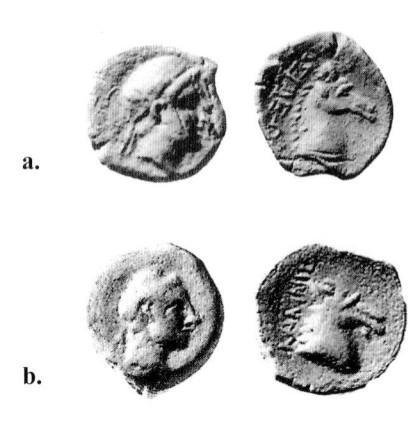

b.

Type 2.4
Obv: Diademed, youthful male head facing right.
Rev: ΒΑΣΙΛΕΩΣ ΚΑΜΝΙΣΚΙΡΟΥ, upright anchor.

Æ Units

    Subtype 1-1   No variation.

    a.

Type 2.5
Obv: Diademed, youthful male head facing right.
Rev: ΒΑΣΙΛΕΩΣ ΚΑΜΝΙΣΚΙΡΟΥ, tripod.

Æ Units

    Subtype 1-1   No variation.

    a.

Type 2.6
Obv: Diademed, youthful male head facing right.
Rev: ΒΑΣΙΛΕΩΣ ΚΑΜΝΙΣΚΙΡΟΥ, cornucopia.

Æ Units

    Subtype 1-1   **Rev:** monogram 3 to right of cornucopia.

    a.

Type 2.7
Obv: Helmeted, youthful male head facing forward.
Rev: ΒΑΣΙΛΕΩΣ ΚΑΜΝΙΣΚΙΡΟΥ, eagle standing right, wings spread.

Æ Units

    Subtype 1-1   No variation.

    a.

Type 2.8
Obv: Diademed, youthful male head facing right.
Rev: ΒΑΣΙΛΕΩΣ ΚΑΜΝΙΣΚΙΡΟΥ, bow and quiver.

Æ Units

    Subtype 1-1   No variation.

a.

Type 2.9
Obv: Helmeted, youthful male head facing right.
Rev: ΒΑΣΙΛΕΩΣ ΚΑΜΝΙΣΚΙΡΟΥ, bow and quiver.

Æ 1/2 Units

    Subtype 1-1   No variation.

a.

Type 2.10
Obv: Helmeted and diademed, youthful male head facing right.
Rev: ΒΑΣΙΛΕΩΣ ΚΑΜΝΙΣΚΙΡΟΥ, Tyche seated left, holding cornucopia in left arm.

Æ Units

    Subtype 1-1   No variation.

a.

Type 2.11
Obv: Helmeted and diademed, youthful male head facing right.
Rev: ΒΑΣΙΛΕΩΣ ΚΑΜΝΙΣΚΙΡΟΥ, Nike standing left, holding wreath in outstretched right hand, palm frond in left hand.

Æ Units

    Subtype 1-1   **Rev:** No variation.

a.

Note on Alram 442: The single example of this coin offers too little evidence for its placement under Elymais.

OKKONAPSES
(Usurper, ca. 144/3 or 139 BC)

Type 3.1
Obv: Diademed, youthful male head facing right; monogram behind; reel and pellet border.
Rev: ΒΑΣΙΛΕΩΣ ΟΚΚΟΝΑΨΟΥ ΣΩΤΗΡΟΣ, youthful god (Belos or Apollo) seated left on an omphalos holding an arrow in his outstretched right hand and a bow in his left hand; pellet border.

  AR Tetradrachms

   Subtype 1-1   **Obv:** monogram 2.

a.

b.

Type 3.2
Obv: Radiate, youthful male head facing right; pellet(?) border.
Rev: ΒΑΣΙΛΕΩΣ ΟΚΚΟΝΑΨΟΥ, youthful god (Belos or Apollo) standing left, leaning on column.

  Æ Units

   Subtype 1-1   No variation.

a.

PHRAATES, SON OF MITHRADATES I
(Arsacid viceroy of Elymais, ca. 139-138 B.C.)

Type 4.1
Obv: Diademed and draped, youthful male bust facing right, with long sideburn; reel and pellet border.
Rev: ΒΑΣΙΛΕΩΣ ΑΡΣΑΚΟΥ, youthful god (Belos or Apollo) seated left on an omphalos, holding an arrow in his outstretched right hand and a bow in his left hand; monogram 5 to outer left, control letters in exergue; pellet border.

AR Tetradrachms

Subtype 1-1   **Rev:** BA in exergue

a.

Subtype 1-2   **Rev:** ΠΤ(?) in exergue

a.

Type 4.2
Obv: Diademed, youthful male head facing right; pellet border.
Rev: ΒΑΣΙΛΕΩΣ ΑΡΣΑΚΟΥ, horse head facing right.

Æ Units

Subtype 1-1   No variation.

a.

Type 4.3
Obv: Diademed, youthful male head facing right; pellet border.
Rev: ΒΑΣΙΛΕΩΖ ΑΡΣΑΚΟΥ, goddess standing left, holding long sceptre; pellet border.

Æ Units

Subtype 1-1   No variation.

a.

Æ 1/2 Units

Subtype 2-1   **Rev:** no variation.

a.

Type 4.4
Obv: Diademed, youthful male head facing right; pellet border.
Rev: ΒΑΣΙΛΕΩΣ ΑΡΣΑΚΟΥ, bull's head facing; pellet border.

Æ Units

Subtype 1-1   **Rev:** no variation.
Note: no photo available of this type.

Type 4.5
Obv: Diademed, youthful male head facing right; pellet border.
Rev: ΒΑΣΙΛΕΩΣ ΑΡΣΑΚΟΥ, Hermes standing left; pellet border.

Æ Units

Subtype 1-1   **Rev:** no variation.
Note: no photo available of this type.

TIGRAIOS
(Usurper, ca. 138/7-133/2 BC)

Type 5.1
Obv: Diademed, youthful male head facing right; monogram behind; reel and pellet border.
Rev: ΒΑΣΙΛΕΩΣ ΤΙΓΡΑΙΟΥ, youthful god (Belos or Apollo) seated left on an omphalos, holding an arrow in his outstretched right hand and a bow in his left hand; pellet border.

AR Tetradrachms

Subtype 1-1   Obv: monogram 3.

a.

Type 5.2
Obv: Diademed, youthful male head facing right; pellet border.
Rev: ΒΑΣΙΛΕΩΣ ΤΙΓΡΑΙΟΥ, Artemis/Ishtar standing left, holding arrow and bow; no border.

Æ Units

Subtype 1-1   No variation.

a.

Type 5.3
Obv: Diademed, youthful male head facing right; pellet border.
Rev: ΒΑΣΙΛΕΩΣ ΤΙΓΡΑΙΟΥ, upright thunderbolt; no border.

Æ Units

Subtype 1-1   No variation.

a.

Type 5.4
Obv: Diademed, youthful male head facing right; pellet border.
Rev: ΒΑΣΙΛΕΩΣ ΤΙΓΡΑΙΟΥ, boar's head left; no border.

Æ Units

    Subtype 1-1   No variation.

a.

Type 5.5
Obv: Helmeted, youthful male head facing right; pellet border.
Rev: ΒΑΣΙΛΕΩΣ ΤΙΓΡΑΙΟΥ, eagle standing right, wings spread; no border.

Æ Units

    Subtype 1-1   No variation.

a.

Type 5.6
Obv: Helmeted, youthful male head facing right; pellet border.
Rev: ΒΑΣΙΛΕΩΣ ΤΙΓΡΑΙΟΥ, herm; no border.

Æ Units

    Subtype 1-1   No variation.

a.

Type 5.7
Obv: Youthful male head facing right, wearing elephant skin headdress; pellet border.
Rev: ΒΑΣΙΛΕΩΣ ΤΙΓΡΑΙΟΥ, palm frond; no border.

Æ Units

    Subtype 1-1   No variation.

a.

b.

DAREIOS
(Usurper, before 129 BC)

Type 6.1
Obv: Diademed, youthful male head facing right; reel and pellet border.
Rev: ΒΑΣΙΛΕΩΣ ΔΑΡΕΙΟΥ ΣΩΤΕΡΟΥ ΝΑΝΑΙΕΝΩΝ, youthful god (Belos or Apollo) seated left on an omphalos, holding an arrow in his outstretched right hand and a bow in his left hand; no border.

AR Tetradrachms

Subtype 1-1   No variation.

a.

LATER KAMNASKIRID DYNASTY

KAMNASKIRES III AND ANZAZE
(Circa 82/1-73/2 BC)

Type 7.1

Obv: Jugate draped busts left of Kamnaskires, diademed, and his queen, Anzaze, wearing stephane; mintmark behind (occasionally overstruck with Nike countermark); reel and pellet or pellet border on some subtypes.

Rev: ΒΑΣΙΛΕΩΣ ΚΑΜΝΑΣΚΙΡΟΥ ΚΑΙ ΒΑΣΙΛΙΣΣΗΣ ΑΝΖΑΖΗΣ, old, bearded god (Belos or Zeus) seated left on throne, holding a small Nike in his outstretched right hand and a sceptre in his left hand; monogram to inner left (on drachms); with or without a date (in various positions); no border.

Notes: The legend on this type has many variations; most often with the Ϲ form for Σ. As this is commonplace, and not indicative of a new type, there is no distinction made.

AR Tetradrachms

Subtype 1-1 Dated S231 or S234 (82/1 or 78/7 BC)
Seleucia on the Hedyphon mint
Obv: anchor mintmark (early form)
Rev: ϹΑΚΕΔΩΝ in small letters reading downward in inner left field; date ΑΛΣ or ΔΛΣ downward in inner right field.

a.

Subtype 1-2 Uncertain date (possibly off flan)
Seleucia on the Hedyphon mint
Obv: anchor mintmark (early form); pellet border.
Rev: ϹΑΚΕΔΩΝ in small letters reading downward in inner left field; uncertain date in exergue(?).

a.

Subtype 1-3 Dated S231 (82/1 BC)
Seleucia on the Hedyphon mint
Obv: anchor mintmark (later form); reel and pellet border.
Rev: uncertain mark to inner left; date ΑΛΣ downward in inner right field.

a.

Subtype 1-4   Dated S233 (80/79 BC)
                    Seleucia on the Hedyphon mint
                    Obv: anchor mintmark (later form); reel and pellet border.
                    Rev: ΣAKEΔΩN in small letters reading downward in inner left field; date ΓΛΣ in exergue.

a.

Subtype 1-5   Dated S237 (76/5 BC)
                    Seleucia on the Hedyphon mint
                    Obv: anchor mintmark (later form); pellet border.
                    Rev: MAKEΔΩN in small letters reading downward in inner left field; date ZΛΣ in exergue.

a.

Subtype 1-6   Undated issue
                    Seleucia on the Hedyphon mint
                    Obv: monogram 6 behind busts; anchor mintmark overstruck with Nike countermark; pellet border.
                    Rev: no date.

a.

AR Drachms

Subtype 2-1A   Dated S234 (79/8 BC)
                    Seleucia on the Hedyphon mint
                    Obv: anchor mintmark.
                    Rev: monogram 7; date ΔΛΣ in exergue.

a.

KAMNASKIRES III and ANZAZE

Subtype 2-1B   Dated S234 (79/8 BC)
Seleucia on the Hedyphon mint
Obv: anchor mintmark.
Rev: monogram 8; date ΔΛΣ in exergue.

a.

Subtype 2-2A   Dated S235 (78/7 BC)
Seleucia on the Hedyphon mint
Obv: anchor mintmark.
Rev: monogram 9; date ΕΛΖ (*sic*) in exergue.

a.

Subtype 2-2B   Dated S235 (78/7 BC)
Seleucia on the Hedyphon mint
Obv: anchor mintmark; pellet border.
Rev: monogram 10; date ΕΛΣ in exergue.

a.

Subtype 2-3   Dated S236 (77/6 BC)
Seleucia on the Hedyphon mint
Obv: anchor mintmark
Rev: monogram 12; date ϛΛΣ downward in inner right field.

a.

Subtype 2-4   Dated S239 (74/3 BC)
Travelling (Court) mint
Obv: no mintmark
Rev: no monogram; date ΘΛΣ in exergue.

a.

b.

Note: These two coins are from the same dies, confirming the lack of a mintmark on the first coin, and date on the second.

Subtype 2-5   Undated issue
Uncertain mint
Obv: mintmark off flan(?); reel and pellet border.
Rev: uncertain monogram, no date.

a.

AR Hemidrachms

Subtype 3-1   Undated issue
Uncertain mint (Susa?)
Obv: monogram 6A in countermark behind busts.
Rev: no monogram.

a.

Subtype 3-2   Undated issue(?)
Travelling (Court) mint
Obv: no mintmark.
Rev: no monogram; date off flan(?).

a.

AR Obols

Subtype 4-1	**Undated issue**
Uncertain mint (Seleucia on the Hedyphon?)
Obv: no mintmark; monogram 6, degraded, behind busts.
Rev: no monogram.

a.

Note: the monogram is also present on type 7.1.1-6, which also has an anchor (later overstruck with the Nike countermark). This would suggest that monogram 1 is associated with Seleucia on the Hedyphon.

Subtype 4-2	**Undated issue**
Susa mint
Obv: anchor behind busts.
Rev: no monogram.

a.

Subtype 4-3	**Undated issue**
Uncertain mint
Obv: no mintmark behind busts.
Rev: degraded legend, no monogram.

a.

KAMNASKIRES IV
(Circa 63/2-54/3 BC)

Type 8.1

Obv: Diademed and draped male bust left, with *young portrait*, and slight or no beard; mintmark behind (occasionally overstruck with Nike countermark); pellet border.

Rev: ΙΑⅭΙΛΕΩⅭ ΚΑΜΝΑⅭΚΙΡΟΥ ΤΟΥ ΕΓ ΒΑⅭΙΛΕΩⅭ ΚΑΜΝΑⅭΚΙΡΟΥ, old, bearded god (Belos or Zeus) seated left on throne, holding a small Nike in his outstretched right hand and a sceptre in his left hand; monogram to inner left; with or without a date in exergue; no border.

Notes: The legend on this type generally translates to "King Kamnaskires, grandson of King Kamnaskires." It has many variations. As this is commonplace, and not indicative of a new type, there is no distinction made.

AR Tetradrachms

Subtype 1-1A   Uncertain date
Seleucia on the Hedyphon mint
Obv: slight beard; anchor mintmark
Rev: monogram 13; date obscured.

a.

Subtype 1-1B   Uncertain date
Seleucia on the Hedyphon mint
Obv: slight beard; anchor mintmark overstruck with Nike countermark.
Rev: monogram 13; date obscured.

a.

AR Drachms

Subtype 2-1   Dated S250 (63/2 BC)
Travelling (Court) mint
Obv: slight beard; no mintmark.
Rev: monogram 13; date ΝΣ.

a.

b.

Subtype 2-2   Uncertain date (undated?)
Travelling (Court) mint
Obv: slight beard; no mintmark.
Rev: monogram 13; date off flan(?).

a.

Subtype 2-3   Undated issue
Travelling (Court) mint
Obv: no beard; no mintmark.
Rev: monogram 13; no date.

a.

b.

AR Obols

Subtype 3-1   Undated issue
Uncertain mint
Obv: no beard; mintmark off flan(?).
Rev: no monogram.

a.

Type 8.2

Obv: Diademed and draped male bust left, with *middle-aged portrait*, and short beard; mintmark behind (occasionally overstruck with Nike countermark); pellet border.

Rev: ΙΑΣΙΛΕΩΣ ΚΑΜΝΑΣΚΙΡΟΥ ΤΟΥ ΕΓ ΒΑΣΙΛΕΩΣ ΚΑΜΝΑΣΚΙΡΟΥ, old, bearded god (Belos or Zeus) seated left on throne, holding a small Nike in his outstretched right hand and a sceptre in his left hand; monogram to inner left; with or without a date in exergue; no border.

Notes: The legend on this type generally translates to "King Kamnaskires, grandson of King Kamnaskires." It has many variations. As this is commonplace, and not indicative of a new type, there is no distinction made.

AR Tetradrachms

Subtype 1-1 Dated S251 or S254 (62/1 or 59/8 BC)
Seleucia on the Hedyphon mint
Obv: anchor mintmark overstruck with Nike countermark.
Rev: monogram 14; date ΑΝΣ or ΔΝΣ.

a.

AR Drachms

Subtype 2-1 Uncertain date (undated?)
Travelling (Court) mint
Obv: no mintmark.
Rev: monogram 13; date off flan(?).

a.

b.

Subtype 2-2 Uncertain date (undated?)
Travelling (Court) mint
Obv: no mintmark.
Rev: monogram 15; date off flan(?).

a.

AR Obols

Subtype 3-1   Undated issue
Uncertain mint
Obv: uncertain mintmark.
Rev: no monogram.

a.

b.

Type 8.3

Obv: Diademed and draped male bust left, with *old portrait*, and full beard; mintmark behind; some with pellet border.
Rev: IAΓIΛEΩΓ KAMNAΓKIPOY TOY EΓ BAΓIΛEΩΓ KAMNAΓKIPOY, old, bearded god (Belos or Zeus) seated left on throne, holding a small Nike in his outstretched right hand and a sceptre in his left hand; monogram to inner left; with or without a date in exergue; no border.
Notes: The legend on this type generally translates to "King Kamnaskires, grandson of King Kamnaskires." It has many variations. As this is commonplace, and not indicative of a new type, there is no distinction made.

AR Tetradrachms

Subtype 1-1   Uncertain date (undated?)
Susa mint
Obv: horse protome mintmark; pellet border.
Rev: monogram 16; date off flan(?).

a.

AR Drachms

Subtype 2-1   Dated S256 (57/6 BC)
Susa mint
Obv: horse head mintmark.
Rev: monogram 16; date ϛNΣ.

a.

b.

c.

d.

Subtype 2-2   Dated S257 (57/6 BC)
Susa mint
Obv: horse protome mintmark; pellet border.
Rev: monogram 16; date ZNΣ.
Note: the dates on this type are often blundered, with readings of ZΠE and ZNE known.

a.

b.

c.

KAMNASKIRES IV

Subtype 2-3   Dated S259 (54/3 BC)
                  Travelling (Court) mint
                  Obv: no mintmark; pellet border.
                  Rev: monogram 16; date ΘΝΣ.

a.

b.

Subtype 2-4   Uncertain date
                  Seleucia on the Hedyphon mint
                  Obv: anchor mintmark.
                  Rev: monogram 17; date off-flan.

a.

AR Hemidrachms

Subtype 3-1   Uncertain date
                  Susa mint
                  Obv: horse head mintmark.
                  Rev: no monogram; date off-flan.

a.

KAMNASKIRES V
(Circa 54/3-33/2 BC)

Type 9.1
Obv: Diademed bust left, with long beard; anchor mintmark behind, usually with symbol (star or rosette above); pellet border.
Rev: ΒΑΣΙΛΕΩΣ ΚΑΜΝΑΣΚΙΡΟΥ ΤΟΥ ΕΓ ΒΑΣΙΛΕΩΣ ΚΑΜΝΑΣΚΙΡΟΥ (usually degraded), diademed, bearded bust left; usually with date (often blundered) in exergue; no border.
Notes: The legend on this type is a continuation of the legend used by his predecessor, Kamnaskires IV. It is uncertain whether its continued use suggests the two may be brothers. However, the legend becomes more degraded over time, suggesting it may have been reused as a matter of convention. Also, the style of the busts on both sides varies greatly.

AR Tetradrachms

Subtype 1-1   Dated S259 (54/3 BC)
Seleucia on the Hedyphon mint
Obv: star above anchor.
Rev: monogram 18 below chin; date ΘΝΣ.

a.

Note: The date on this particular coin is unclear. Senior (1998) dated the coin ΘΛΣ (S239 = 74/3 BC), but this is too early in comparison with dates on all other coins of this type. The style and fabric also argue for a later date. A close inspection of the coin supports a reading of ΘΝΣ (S 259 = 53/2 BC).

Subtype 1-2   Dated S265 (48/7 BC)
Seleucia on the Hedyphon mint
Obv: star above anchor.
Rev: date ΕΞΣ.

a.

Subtype 1-3   Dated S266 (47/6 BC)
Seleucia on the Hedyphon mint
Obv: star above anchor.
Rev: date ϛΞΣ (retrograde).

a.

Subtype 1-4 Dated S267 (46/5 BC)
Seleucia on the Hedyphon mint
Obv: star above anchor.
Rev: date ZΞΣ (retrograde).

a.

Subtype 1-5A Dated S277 (36/5 BC)
Seleucia on the Hedyphon mint
Obv: star above anchor.
Rev: monogram 18 to lower left; date ZOΣ (retrograde).

a.

Subtype 1-5B Dated S277 (36/5 BC)
Seleucia on the Hedyphon mint
Obv: symbol and mintmark off flan.
Rev: monogram 20 to upper left; date ΣOZ.

a.

Subtype 1-6 Dated S280 (33/2 BC)
Seleucia on the Hedyphon mint
Obv: star above anchor.
Rev: date ΠΣ.

a.

Subtype 1-7 Uncertain date
 Seleucia on the Hedyphon mint
 Obv: star above anchor.
 Rev: date obscured or off flan; sometimes with monogram.

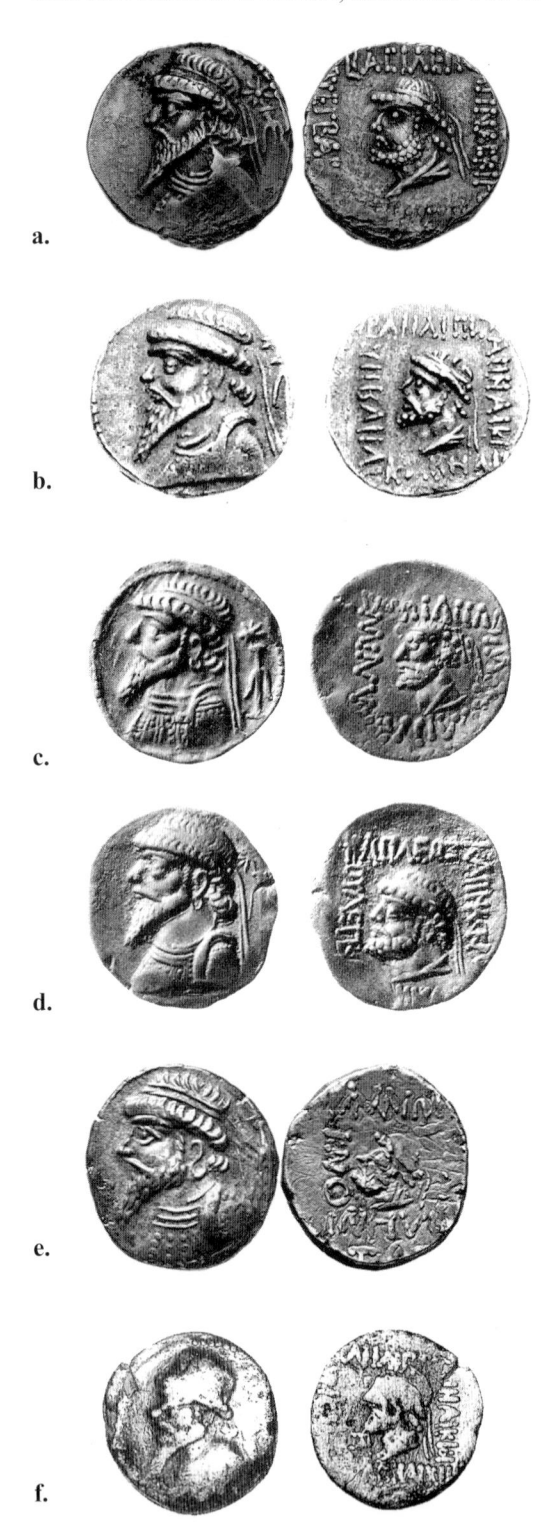

a.

b.

c.

d.

e.

f.

Note: this specimen has an uncertain monogram on the reverse.

KAMNASKIRES V

g.

Note: although the style varies throughout the series, as evidenced by the dated issues above, this and the following two coins of uncertain date displays characteristics (highly degraded reverse style and legends) that are very similar to the early issues of the early Arsacid kings (Type 10, below). It must be among the last issues of Kamnaskires V's reign.

h.

i.

AR or Bl Drachms

Subtype 2-1   Dated S262 (51/0 BC)
Seleucia on the Hedyphon mint
Obv: star above anchor.
Rev: date ΒΞΣ (?).

a.

b.

Subtype 2-2	**Dated S267 (46/5 BC)** **Seleucia on the Hedyphon mint** **Obv:** symbol and mintmark off flan. **Rev:** date ZΞΣ.

a.

Note: the date on this specimen is retrograde.

Subtype 2-3	**Dated S271 (42/1 BC)** **Seleucia on the Hedyphon mint** **Obv:** star above anchor. **Rev:** monogram 19 to lower left; date ΑΟΣ.

a.

Subtype 2-4A	**Dated S277 (36/5 BC)** **Seleucia on the Hedyphon mint** **Obv:** star above anchor. **Rev:** date ZOΣ.

a.

Subtype 2-4B	**Dated S277 (36/5 BC)** **Seleucia on the Hedyphon mint** **Obv:** anchor with no symbol above. **Rev:** date ZOΣ.

a.

Note: The date on this specimen is retrograde.

Subtype 2-4C   Dated S277 (36/5 BC)
Seleucia on the Hedyphon mint
Obv: symbol and mintmark obscured or off flan.
Rev: date ZOΣ.

a.

Note: The date on this specimen is engraved as OΣZ.

Subtype 2-5   Undated
Seleucia on the Hedyphon mint
Obv: star above anchor.
Rev: no date.

a.

Subtype 2-6A   Uncertain date
Seleucia on the Hedyphon mint
Obv: star above anchor.
Rev: date obscured or off flan.

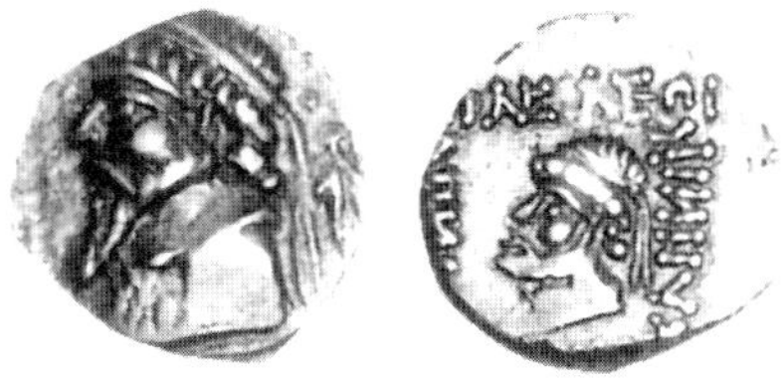

a.

b.

Subtype 2-6B   Uncertain date
Seleucia on the Hedyphon mint
Obv: star above anchor.
Rev: date obscured or off flan; monogram 19 to inner left.

a.

AR or BI Hemidrachms

Subtype 3-1   Dated S267 (46/5 BC)
Seleucia on the Hedyphon mint
Obv: star above anchor.
Rev: date ZΞΣ.

a.

Subtype 3-2   Uncertain date
Seleucia on the Hedyphon mint
Obv: anchor mintmark without symbol above.
Rev: date off flan(?).

a.

Subtype 3-3   Uncertain date
Seleucia on the Hedyphon mint(?)
Obv: no mintmark.
Rev: date off flan(?).

a.

Subtype 3-4   Uncertain date
Seleucia on the Hedyphon mint(?)
Obv: uncertain mintmark.
Rev: date off flan(?).

a.

b.

AR or BI Obols

Subtype 4-1 Uncertain date
Seleucia on the Hedyphon mint
Obv: star above anchor.
Rev: date off flan(?).

a.

Subtype 4-2 Undated issue
Seleucia on the Hedyphon mint(?)
Obv: no mintmark.
Rev: no date.

a.

AR or BI Hemiobols

Subtype 5-1 Uncertain date
Seleucia on the Hedyphon mint(?)
Obv: no mintmark.
Rev: date obscured.

a.

Type 9.2

Obv: Diademed bust left, with long beard; anchor mintmark behind, usually with symbol (star or rosette above); pellet border.
Rev: BAΣIΛEΩΣ KAMNAΣKIPOY TOY EΓ BAΣIΛEΩΣ KAMNAΣKIPOY (usually degraded), diademed, bearded bust right; usually with date (often blundered) in exergue; no border.
Notes: As with Type 9.1, the legend on this type is a continuation of the legend used by his predecessor, Kamnaskires IV. It is uncertain whether this suggests the two may be brothers. However, the legend on the sole example of this type (below) is degraded, suggesting it may have been reused as a matter of convention.

AR or BI Drachms

Subtype 1-1 Dated S277 (36/5 BC)
Seleucia on the Hedyphon mint
Obv: star above anchor mintmark.
Rev: date ZOΣ.

a.

Elymais Arsacid Dynasty

Uncertain Early Arsacid Kings
(Late 1st century B.C. – early 2nd century A.D.)

The coinage of these kings is quite complicated. As noted in Part I, the reverse type goes through a transformation, from a well-styled bust within a rudimentary legend based on the coinage of the last Kamnaskirid king (Type 9). It is clear that these coins span about a century's time, and therefore must be from more than one king. As such, although the basic type, obverse bust left and reverse bust in legend, remains constant (albeit gradually degrading), the coinage is broken into more than one type. The primary subdivision is based on the symbol above the anchor, which appears to have a relative chronology of: rosette, rosette-in-crescent, star-in-crescent, and, finally, dot-in-crescent. These subdivisions are then further divided by the stage of degeneration of the reverse.

Type 10.1
Obv: Bust of decent style left, with long, curly, pointed beard, and curly hair dressed in a curved pattern from forehead to the nape of the neck, topped by a tuft of hair bound with a diadem, its ties falling behind; behind, *rosette above anchor* with one or two crossbars; sometimes a pellet to left of the anchor; pellet border.
Rev: Diademed, bearded head left, of decent style; degraded legend around, forming square frame around the head; no border.

Æ Tetradrachms

Subtype 1-1   **Obv:** anchor with two crossbars; pellet to left of anchor.

a.

b.

Æ Drachms

Subtype 2-1   **Obv:** anchor with two crossbars; no pellet.

a.

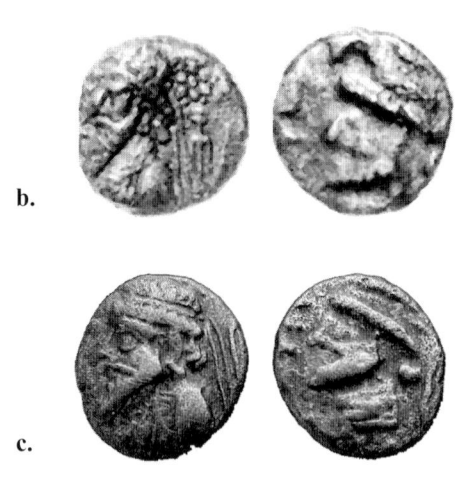

b.

c.

Note: although the rosette is off the flan on this example, the style is nearly identical with the previous coin.

Subtype 2-2   Obv: anchor with one crossbar; no pellet.

a.

Note: Hansman (1990) thought the letters in front of the bust of this coin were the date ΤΠΔ (S384 = AD 71/2).

Type 10.2
Obv: Bust of decent style left, with long, curly, pointed beard, and curly hair dressed in a curved pattern from forehead to the nape of the neck, topped by a tuft of hair bound with a diadem, its ties falling behind; behind, *rosette in crescent above anchor* with one or two crossbars; a pellet to left of anchor; pellet border
Rev: Diademed, bearded head left, of decent style; degraded legend around, forming square frame around the head; no border.

Æ Tetradrachms

Subtype 1-1   Obv: anchor with two crossbars; pellet to left of anchor.

a.

b.

Type 10.3

Obv: Bust of varying style left, with long, curly, pointed beard, and curly hair dressed in a curved pattern from forehead to the nape of the neck, topped by a tuft of hair bound with a diadem, its ties falling behind; behind, *star in crescent above anchor* with one or two crossbars; sometimes a pellet to the left, right, or above the anchor; pellet border.

Rev: Diademed, bearded head left, of varying style; degraded legend around, forming square frame around the head; no border.

Note: During the course of this very long-lasting type, the style gradually degrades; the star morphs into a cross-like form, the head on the reverse changes from a crude to totally degenerated form, and the legend becomes more blundered. ***The degeneration of the reverse type is the primary determination for the division of the subtypes.***

Æ Tetradrachms

Subtype 1-1A   **Rev:** decent style bust.
  Obv: anchor with two crossbars; no pellet.

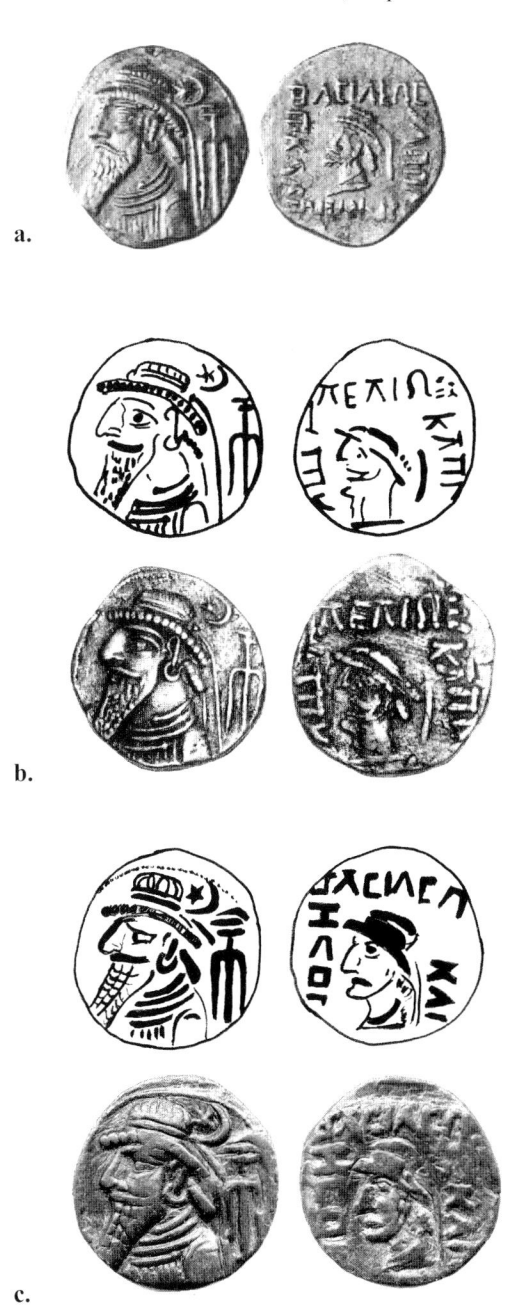

a.

b.

c.

d.

Note: On this example, the lower portion of the pellet border has been changed into a line below the bust.

Subtype 1-1B   **Rev:** crude style bust.
Obv: anchor with two crossbars; pellet to left of anchor.

a.

b.

Subtype 1-1C   **Rev:** crude style bust.
Obv: anchor with two crossbars; pellet above anchor.

a.

UNCERTAIN EARLY ARSACID KINGS

b.

Subtype 1-1D Rev: crude style bust.
Obv: anchor with two crossbars; pellet to right of anchor.

a.

b.

Subtype 1-2A Rev: highly degenerated bust.
Obv: anchor with two crossbars; pellet to left of anchor.

a.

Subtype 1-2B **Rev:** highly degenerated bust.
Obv: anchor with one crossbar; no pellet.

a.

Æ Drachms

Subtype 2-1 **Obv:** anchor with one crossbar; pellet to left of anchor.

a.

b.

c.

Type 10.4

Obv: Bust of decent style left, with long, curly, pointed beard, and curly hair dressed in a curved pattern from forehead to the nape of the neck, topped by a tuft of hair bound with a diadem, its ties falling behind; behind, ***pellet in crescent*** above anchor with one or two crossbars; sometimes a pellet to left of or above anchor; pellet border.
Rev: Diademed, bearded head left, of rudimentary to completely degraded style; degraded legend around, forming square frame around the head; no border.
Note: As with the star-in-crescent type (10.3), the style of this type becomes more crude over time. While the obverse has insignificant changes, the reverse begins as a rudimentary outline form that degrades first into a featureless outline, then totally degrades into a rough form of dashes. At the same time, the legend also becomes more degenerate, and gradually joins with the degenerated bust. ***The degeneration of the reverse type is the primary determination for the division of the subtypes.***

Æ Tetradrachms

Subtype 1-1 **Obv:** anchor with two crossbars; no pellet.
Rev: rudimentary style.

a.

b.

Subtype 1-2 **Obv:** anchor with two crossbars; no pellet.
Rev: crude style.

a.

Æ Drachms

Subtype 2-1A **Obv:** anchor with two crossbars; no pellet.
Rev: rudimentary style.

a.

b.

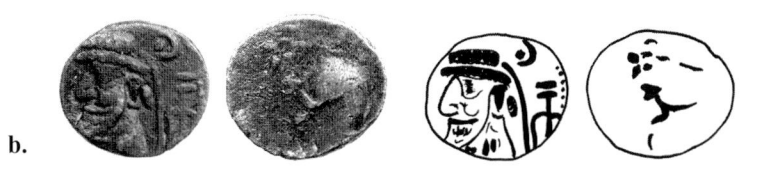

Note: The reverse of this coin was struck with a broken reverse die; the style is not clearly reflected by this example.

Subtype 2-1B   **Obv**: anchor with two crossbars; pellet to left of anchor.
Rev: rudimentary style.

a.

Subtype 2-2A   **Obv**: anchor with two crossbars; pellet above anchor.
Rev: crude style.

a.

b.

Subtype 2-2B   **Obv**: anchor with one crossbar; pellet to left of anchor.
Rev: rudimentary style.

a.

b.

UNCERTAIN EARLY ARSACID KINGS

Subtype 2-3   **Obv:** anchor with one crossbar; no pellet.
Rev: highly degenerated style.

a.

b.

Subtype 2-4A   **Obv:** anchor with one crossbar; no pellet.
Rev: type degenerated to dashes of regular or irregular style.

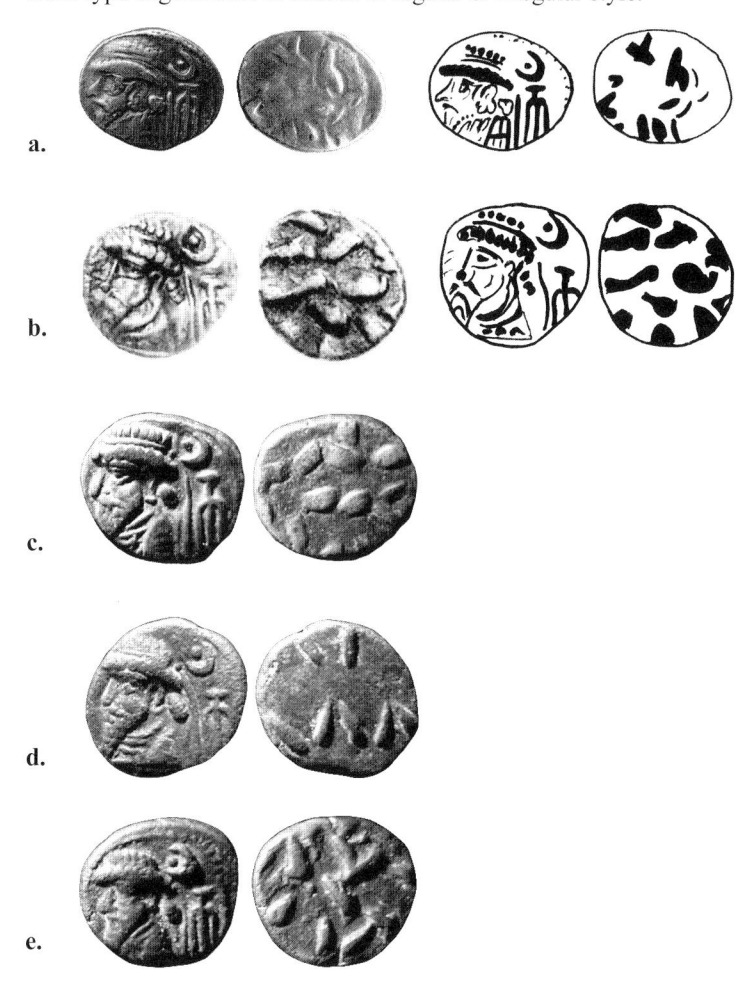

a.

b.

c.

d.

e.

Subtype 2-4B   **Obv:** anchor with one crossbar; pellet above anchor.
Rev: type degenerated to dashes.

a.

ORODES I
(Late 1ˢᵗ – early 2ⁿᵈ centuries A.D.)

Type 11.1
Obv: Bust left, with long, pointed beard, and hair dressed in Parthian fashion, with a large tuft behind the face extending to the back of the head, topped by a tuft bound with a diadem, its ties falling behind; in field before, Aramaic legend; behind, star within crescent above anchor with one or two crossbars; pellet border.
Rev: Diademed head left of *rudimentary style*; degraded legend around, forming square frame around the head; no border.
Note: On the coins, the legend generally appears as such:

Æ Tetradrachms

    Subtype 1-1   **Obv:** with legend; anchor with two crossbars.

a.

b.

c.

d.

    Subtype 1-2   **Obv:** with legend; anchor with one crossbar.

a.

b.

Type 11.2

Obv: Bust left, with long, pointed beard, and hair dressed in Parthian fashion, with a large tuft behind the face extending to the back of the head, topped by a tuft bound with a diadem, its ties falling behind; behind, star within crescent above anchor with one or two crossbars; pellet border.

Rev: Diademed head left of *rudimentary style*; degraded legend around, forming square frame around the head; no border.

Æ Tetradrachms

Subtype 1-1   Obv: no legend; anchor with two crossbars.

a.

b.

Subtype 1-2   Obv: no legend; anchor with one crossbar.

a.

KAMNASKIRES-ORODES
(Early-mid 2nd century A.D.)

The coinage of this king is quite plentiful, and as noted in Part I, has an obverse that breaks from the precedent of the previous reigns, in that it displays a forward facing bust. Within the three types that are identified for this king, there are apparently two primary subdivisions based on the presence or absence of a small hair tuft on the top of the bust on the obverse. The relative chronology of these two subdivisions is set by the first series, where all of the busts without the tuft have a reverse type of a degenerated bust within legend, which is most similar to those of the previous kings (Types 10 and 11). In contrast, while this reverse type is also paired with the obverses with tuft, the vast majority of these obverses are paired with reverses of dashes in irregular and regular patterns, which is most similar to those of the reigns following this king.

Type 12.1

Obv: Large or small diademed bust facing forward, *with or without small hair tuft on top*, and large curly hair tufts on each side *of upward- or horizontally oriented rows*; to left, Aramaic legend running counter clockwise from above; to right, star within crescent above anchor with two or three crossbars; sometimes a dot or dot above symbol (resembling a lion's head) between bust and anchor; pellet border.
Rev: Dashes in regular or irregular pattern, or highly degraded bust within legend; no border.
Note: The legend has two forms that vary in the first name. Their letters tend to stray from proper epigraphic form, and typically appear as such:

Legend 1	kbnhzkyr wrwd MLK' BR wrwd MLK' *King Kamnaskires-Orodes, son of King Orodes*
Legend 2	kbnhkyr wrwd MLK' BR wrwd MLK' *King Kamnaskir-Orodes, son of King Orodes*

After Alram (1986)

Æ Tetradrachms

Subtype 1-1A   **Obv:** bust without hair tuft on top, horizontally-oriented tufts on sides; legend 1; anchor with two crossbars.
Rev: highly degraded bust within legend.

a.

b.

Subtype 1-1B Obv: bust without hair tuft on top, horizontally-oriented tufts on sides; dot and symbol between bust and anchor; legend 1.
Rev: highly degraded bust within legend.

a.

Subtype 1-1C Obv: bust without hair tuft on top, horizontally-oriented tufts on sides; dot and symbol between bust and anchor; legend 2.
Rev: highly degraded bust within legend.

a.

Subtype 1-2 Obv: bust with hair tuft on top and upward-oriented tufts on sides; legend 1; anchor with two crossbars; dot above symbol between bust and anchor.
Rev: highly degraded bust within legend.
Note: this subtype is transitional, with the obverse symbol and reverse type of the previous subtype, and the hair tuft of the following subtype.

a.

b.

Subtype 1-3A Obv: bust with hair tuft on top and upward-oriented tufts on sides; legend 1; anchor with two crossbars.
Rev: irregular pattern of dashes.

a.

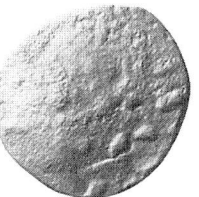

Subtype 1-3B **Obv:** bust with hair tuft on top and upward-oriented tufts on sides; legend 1; anchor with two crossbars; dot between bust and anchor.
Rev: irregular pattern of dashes.

a.

Subtype 1-3C **Obv:** bust with hair tuft on top and upward-oriented tufts on sides; legend 2; anchor with two crossbars.
Rev: regular pattern of dashes.

a.

Subtype 1-3D **Obv:** bust with hair tuft on top and upward-oriented tufts on sides; legend 2; anchor with two crossbars; dot between bust and anchor.
Rev: regular pattern of dashes.

a.

b.

c.

Note: typically, the regular pattern of dashes is in parallel lines, but here the pattern appears to be an intentional design of a six-point star within a circle of dashes with dashes radiating outward from the circle.

Subtype 1-3E **Obv:** bust with hair tuft on top and upward-oriented tufts on sides; legend 2; anchor with two crossbars; dot between bust and anchor.
Rev: irregular pattern of dashes.

a.

Subtype 1-3F **Obv:** bust with hair tuft on top and upward-oriented tufts on sides; legend 2; anchor with three crossbars; dot between bust and anchor.
Rev: regular pattern of dashes.

a.

Note: the hair tufts on the sides of the head on this coin is unusually large, with ten rows.

Type 12.2

Obv: Diademed bust facing forward, *with or without small hair tuft on top*, and large curly hair tufts on each side *of upward- or horizontally-oriented rows*; to right, pellet within crescent above anchor with *two or three crossbars*; pellet border.
Rev: Radiate bust of Belos facing forward, with large hair tufts, *sometimes nimbate*, on each side, two horns, and tied hair on top of the head; Aramaic legend around, starting at varying points, reading counter clockwise; pellet border. *There are multiple minor varieties of the reverse style and legend, not all are illustrated below.*
Note: The legend sometimes has extra letters. Also, the letters in the legend tend to stray from proper epigraphic form, and generally appear as such:

> ܐܢܡܟܝܪ ܘܪܘܕ ܡܠܟܐ
> **knmkyr wrwd MLK'**
> *King Kamnaskires-Orodes*

Æ Drachms

Subtype 1-1A **Obv:** bust without small hair tuft on top and horizontal side tufts; three crossbars on anchor.
Rev: hair tuft on top of bust.

a.

b.

Subtype 1-1B Obv: bust without small hair tuft on top and horizontal side tufts; two crossbars on anchor.
Rev: small hair tuft on top of bust.

a.

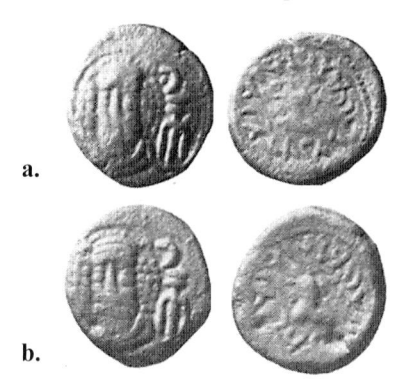

b.

Subtype 1-1C Obv: bust without small hair tuft on top and horizontal side tufts; two crossbars on anchor.
Rev: large hair tuft on top of bust.

a.

b.

c.

Note: this particular piece also has two extra letters in the legend, which also starts on the right, rather than above.

Subtype 1-1D Obv: bust without small hair tuft on top and horizontal side tufts; two crossbars on anchor.
Rev: small hair tuft on top of bust.

a.

Note: the legend this particular piece starts on the lower right, rather than above.

b.

Subtype 1-1E   **Obv:** bust without small hair tuft on top and upward side tufts; two crossbars on anchor.
Rev: no hair tuft on top of bust, side tufts of 6 dots.

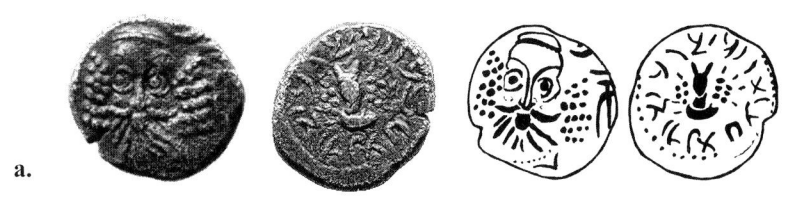

a.

Note: this particular piece also has two extra letters in the legend, which also starts on the right, rather than above.

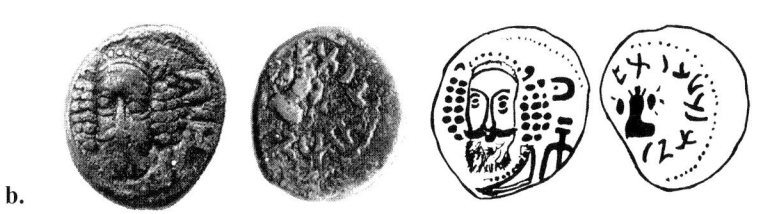

Subtype 1-2A   **Obv:** bust with small hair tuft on top and upward-oriented tufts on sides; two crossbars on anchor.
Rev: bust with heavy hair tufts with rayed nimbus.

a.   bust on rev.

b.

Subtype 1-2B   **Obv:** bust with small hair tuft on top and upward-oriented tufts on sides; two crossbars on anchor.
Rev: bust with hair tufts of small dots, with no nimbus.

a.   bust on rev.

b.

Type 12.3

Obv: Diademed bust facing forward of varying size, *with or without small hair tuft on top*, and large curly hair tufts on each side *of upward- or horizontally-oriented rows*; to right, pellet within crescent above anchor with *one or two* crossbars; sometimes a pellet or uncertain symbol between bust and anchor; pellet border.

Rev: Dashes, with or without regular pattern; no border.

Note: As with the other types of this king, there are two primary subdivisions within this type based on the presence of the hair tuft on the obverse bust. These are divisions are further divided by the form of the side hair tufts, and then the number of crossbars on the anchor.

The regularity or irregularity of the pattern of dashes is not synchronous with the various subtypes differentiated by characteristics of the obverse. As such, the reverses have no bearing on the identification of the subtypes, and they are not included in the illustrations below. For orientation purposes, a variety of these reverses are illustrated below:

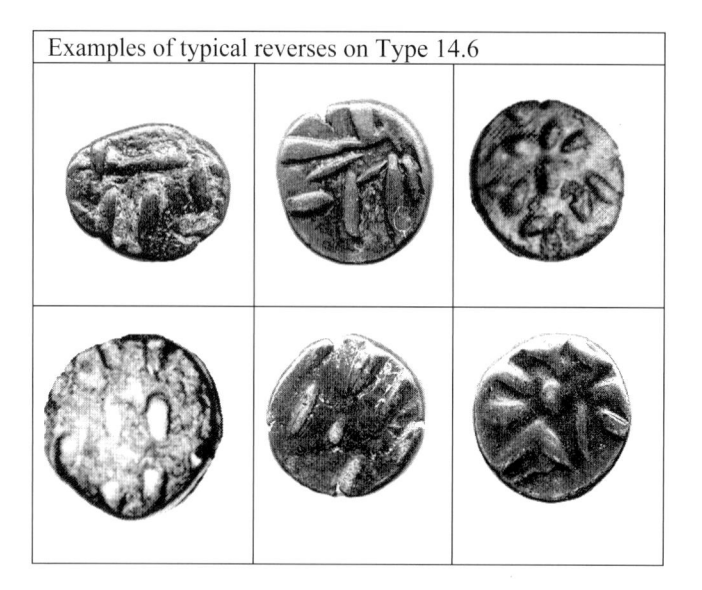

| Examples of typical reverses on Type 14.6 |

Æ Drachms

    Subtype 1-1A   **Obv:** bust without top hair tuft; horizontal side tufts; two crossbars on anchor.

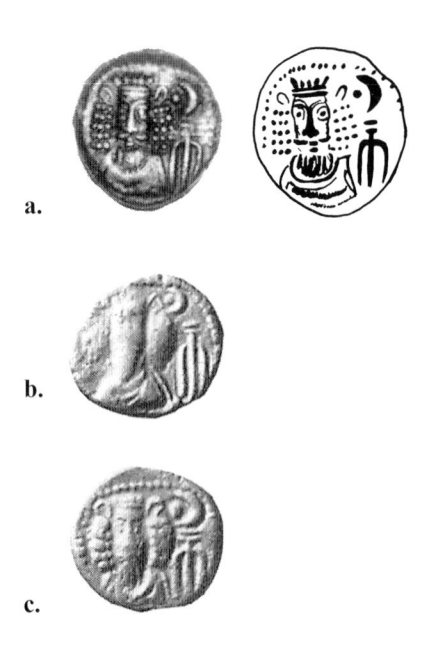

a.

b.

c.

Subtype 1-1B   Obv: bust without top hair tuft; horizontal side tufts; one crossbar on anchor.

a.

b.

c.

d.

Note: coins b, c, and d have an unusual amount (three) of diadem bands.

e.

Note: this and the following example have a small symbol between the bust and anchor.

f.

Subtype 1-2A1   Obv: bust with top hair tuft; upward side tufts; two crossbars on anchor.

a.

b.

c.

Note: this and the following two examples have a pellet between the bust and anchor.

d.

e.

Subtype 1-2A2   Obv: bust with top hair tuft; upward side tufts; one crossbar on anchor.

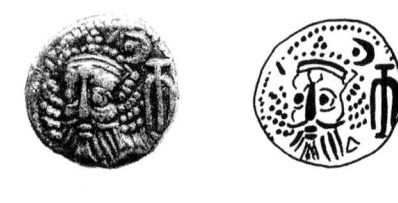

a.

b.

c.

d.

KAMNASKIRES-ORODES 103

e.

Note: this and the following two examples have a pellet between the bust and anchor.

f.

g.

Subtype 1-2B1 **Obv:** bust with top hair tuft; horizontal side tufts; two crossbars on anchor.

a.

b.

c.

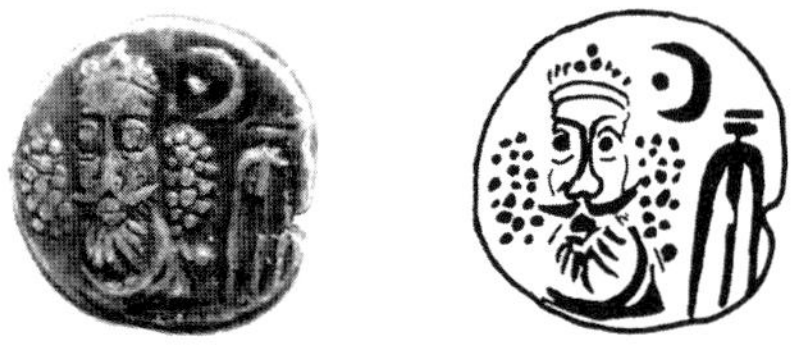

d.

Note: this and the following two examples have a pellet between the bust and anchor.

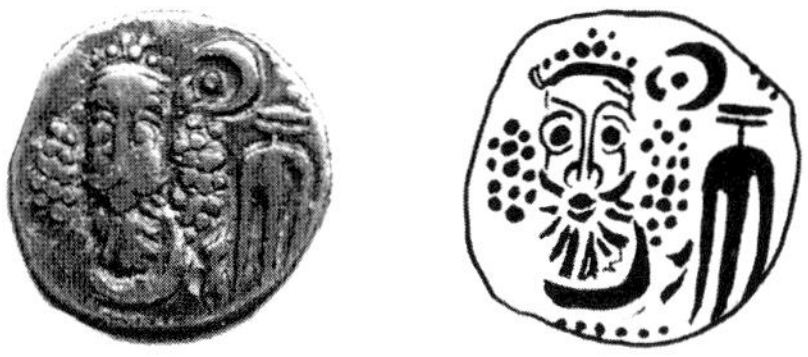

e.

f.

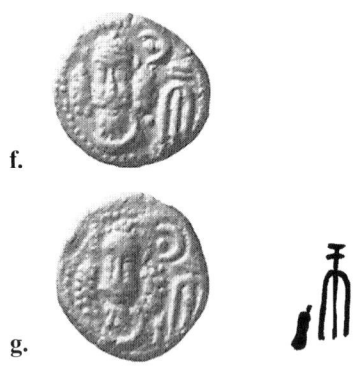

g.

Note: this example has a small symbol between the bust and anchor.

Subtype 1-2B2 **Obv:** bust with top hair tuft; horizontal side tufts; one crossbar on anchor.

a.

b.

Note: this and the following example have a pellet between the bust and anchor.

c.

d.

Note: this and the following example have a small symbol between the bust and anchor.

e.

Type 12.4

Obv: Diademed bust facing forward, ***without small hair tuft on top***, and large curly hair tufts on each side ***of upward-oriented rows***; to right, pellet within crescent above anchor with ***one*** crossbar; pellet border.

Rev: Bearded bust left; circular Aramaic legend around.

Note: De Morgan cited a coin in his personal collection as the sole example of this type. He read the legend as similar to Type 12.2 above. This coin appeared in the supplemental plates in Hill (BMC, pl. LIII [illustrated below]). Alram notes that the reverse is too crude to verify De Morgan's description.

AR Drachm

Subtype 1-1   No variation.

a.

ORODES II
(Early-mid 2nd century AD)

Type 13.1

Obv: Diademed bust facing forward, sometimes with small hair tuft on top, and large curly hair tufts on each side in upward- or horizontally-oriented rows; to right, pellet within crescent above anchor with ***one or two*** crossbars; pellet border.

Rev: Radiate bust of Belos facing forward, with large hair tufts on each side, two horns, and tied hair on top of the head; Aramaic legend around, starting at varying points, reading counter clockwise; pellet border. ***There are many minor variations of the reverse that are not indicative of further subtypes; not all are illustrated below.***

Note: This is a ***transitional*** type with an obverse in the style of Kamnaskires-Orodes and a reverse with the legend King Orodes Son of Orodes. The legend sometimes is blundered or has extra letters. Also, the letters in the legend tend to stray from proper epigraphic form, and generally appear as such:

ʼיЧי ıуכ ـyJx ʼИЧי	**WRWD MLK' BRY WRWD** *King Orodes, Son of Orodes*

Æ Drachms

Subtype 1-1   **Obv:** side tufts in two vertical rows of dots; two crossbars on anchor.

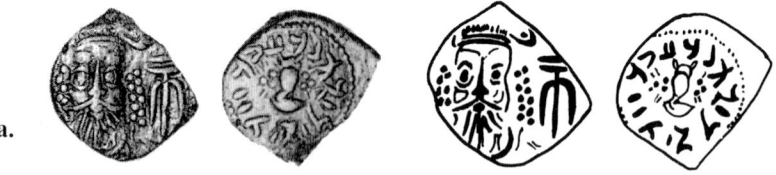

a.

Note: on this example, the legend begins on the lower right.

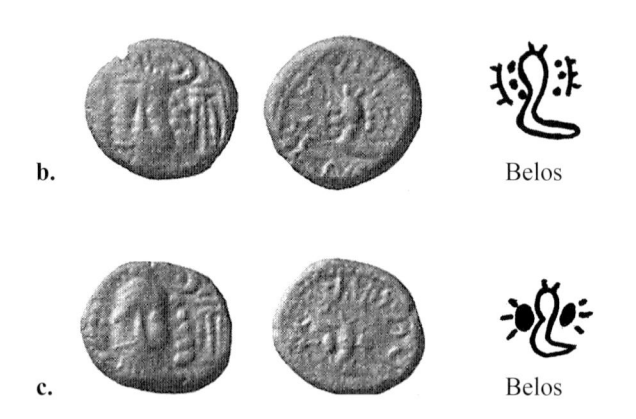

b.   Belos

c.   Belos

Subtype 1-2   **Obv:** side tufts in 3 or more rows, oriented upwards; one crossbar on anchor.

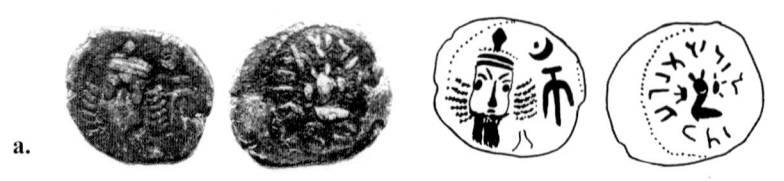

a.

Note: on this example, the legend begins on the right.

ORODES II

107

b.

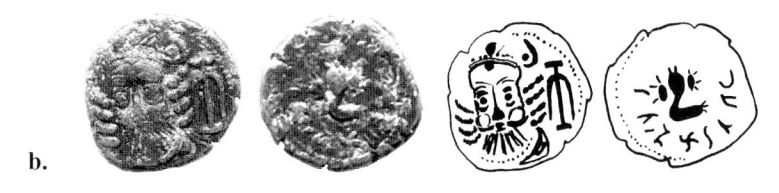

Note: on this example, the legend begins on the left.

c.

Note: on this example, the legend begins on the right.

d. Belos

e.

Note: on this example, the legend begins on the upper left.

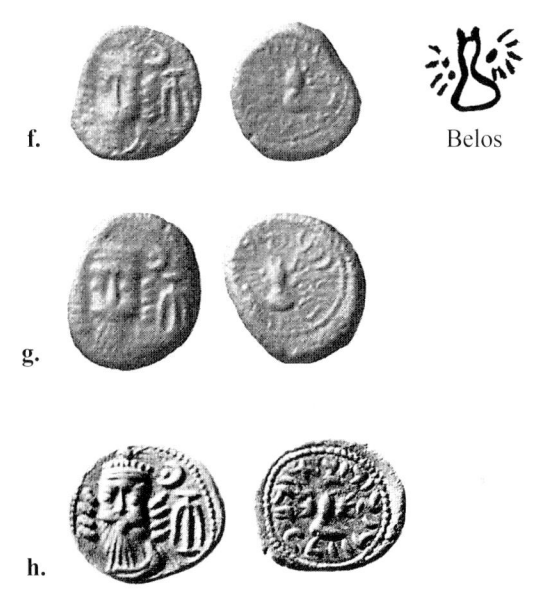

f. Belos

g.

h.

Note: on this example, the legend begins on the right.

Type 13.2

Obv: Bust facing forward, with no large hair tufts at sides, wearing tiara (sometimes crested) usually with central vertical line and dots at rim, diadem band below tiara; to right, dot within crescent above anchor with *one or two crossbars* at top; pellet border.

Rev: Radiate bust of Belos facing forward, with hair tufts on each side and two horns; Aramaic legend around, starting at varying points, reading counter clockwise; pellet border.

Note: The Aramaic legend is frequently corrupted or incomplete, but generally should appear as such:

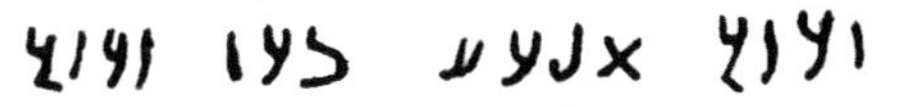 ΥΙΥΙ ΙΥϽ ͺΥͺͻx ΥΙΥΙ	**URUD MALKA BARI URUD** *King Orodes, Son of Orodes*

Æ Drachms

Subtype 1-1A **Obv:** two crossbars on anchor.
Rev: large bust with facial features, calathus, and hair tufts with three protruding dotted rays.

a.

Subtype 1-1B **Obv:** two crossbars on anchor.
Rev: small bust with no facial features, and hair tufts with three protruding dotted rays.

a.

b.

Note: the obverse tiara on this example has a crest.

Subtype 1-2A **Obv:** one crossbar on anchor; wide or slender bust.
Rev: large bust with facial features and calathus.

a.

b.

c.

d.

Subtype 1-2B Obv: one crossbar on anchor; wide or slender bust.
Rev: small bust with no facial features.

a.

b.

c.

Note: the legend is retrograde on this example.

d.

Note: the obverse on this example has a dot below the anchor.

e.

110 ORODES II

f.

Note: the tiara on coins f - i are crested.

g.

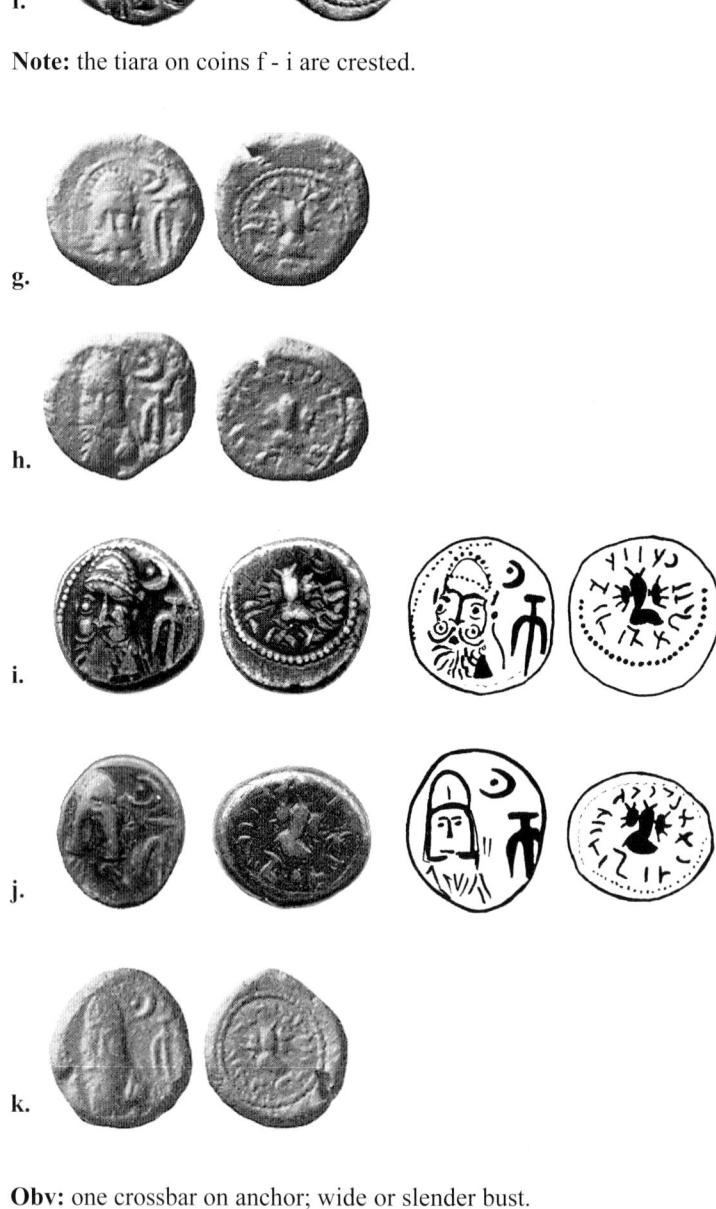

h.

i.

j.

k.

Subtype 1-2C **Obv:** one crossbar on anchor; wide or slender bust.
Rev: small bust with no facial features; corrupt legend.

a.

b.

c.

d.

e.

Note: the obverse on this example has a dot below the anchor.

Type 13.3

Obv: Bust facing forward, wearing tiara, sometimes crested, with central vertical line and dots at rim, two or three diadem bands below tiara, sometimes with row of pearls; to left on tetradrachms, Aramaic legend; to right, star within crescent above anchor with two crossbars at top, and, on tetradrachms, one, two, or no crossbars at bottom; pellet border.

Rev: Dashes with regular pattern; no border.

Note: The legend on the tetradrachms runs *left to right* and generally appears as such:

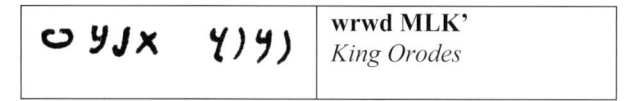

⊃ yJx y)y)	wrwd MLK'
	King Orodes

Also, the pattern of dashes on the reverse is not synchronous with the various subtypes differentiated by characteristics of the obverse. As such, the reverses have no bearing on the identification of the subtypes, and are not included in the illustrations below. For orientation purposes, examples of typical reverses are illustrated below:

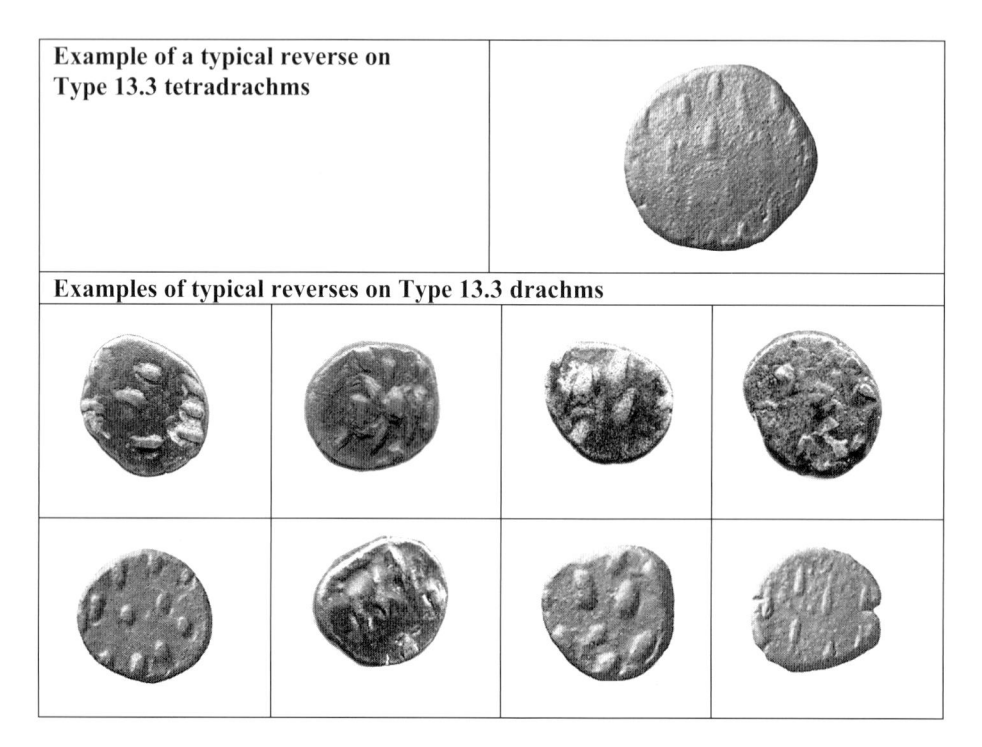

Example of a typical reverse on Type 13.3 tetradrachms	
Examples of typical reverses on Type 13.3 drachms	

Æ Tetradrachms

Subtype 1-1   **Obv:** two diadem bands without row of pearls; small domelike tiara; two crossbars at bottom of anchor.

a.

Subtype 1-2	**Obv:** two diadem bands without row of pearls; tall conical tiara; one crossbar at bottom of anchor.

a.

b.

Subtype 1-3A	**Obv:** two diadem bands with row of pearls; one crossbar at bottom of anchor.

a.

Subtype 1-3B	**Obv:** two diadem bands with row of pearls; two crossbars at bottom of anchor.

a.

Subtype 1-3C	**Obv:** two diadem bands with row of pearls; no crossbar at bottom of anchor.

a.

Subtype 1-4	**Obv:** three diadem bands; one crossbar at bottom of anchor.

a.

Æ Drachms

Subtype 2-1A Obv: Two crossbars on anchor; tiara without crest.

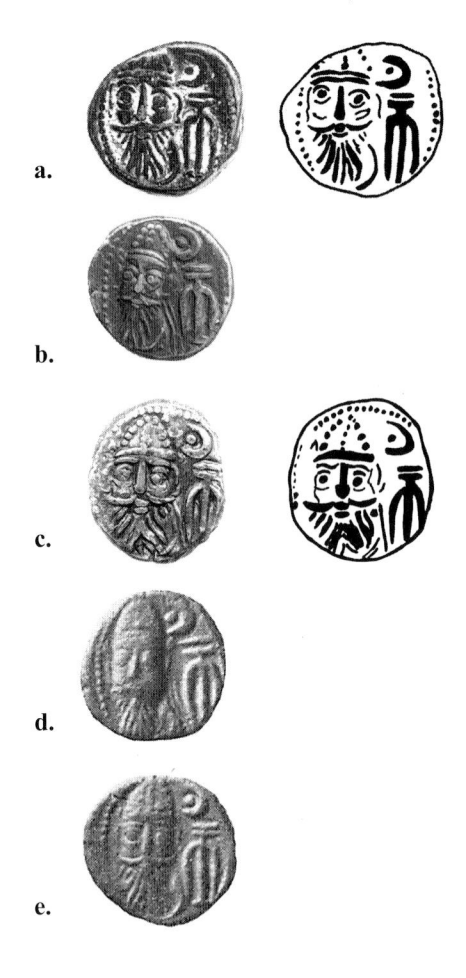

a.

b.

c.

d.

e.

Subtype 2-1B Obv: Two crossbars on anchor; tiara with crest.

a.

b.

Subtype 2-2A Obv: One crossbar on anchor; tiara without crest.

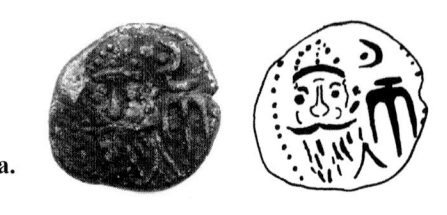

a.

ORODES II 115

b.

c.

d.

e.

f.

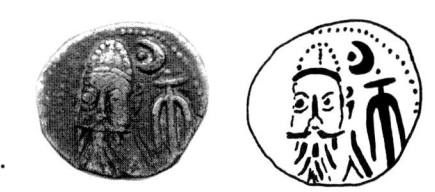

g.

Note: This example has a pellet above the anchor.

Subtype 2-2B   Obv: One crossbar on anchor; tiara with crest **of rays**.

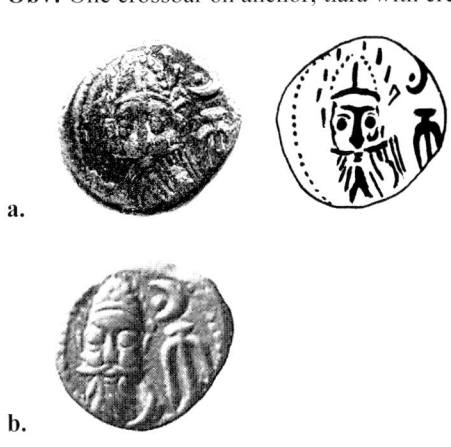

a.

b.

ORODES II

c.

d.

e.

Subtype 2-2C   **Obv:** One crossbar on anchor; tiara with crest of dots.

a.

PHRAATES
(Early-mid 2nd century AD)

The differentiating feature for Phraates' coins is the decoration of the tiara with one or two pellet-in-crescents. This feature, however, is not always visible, and it is possible to confuse these coins with those of Orodes I. For Augé (following de la Fuÿe 1919) this is reason to classify these coins as being of uncertain origin. He also argues – less convincingly, based on his examples – that the bulging style of Orodes' eyes can distinguish these coins from the proper Phraates coins. In this catalogue I have not followed Augé, and assigned to Phraates all coins with the reverse types diadem, eagle, or scattered crescents (Types 14.2-5).

Type 14.1

Obv: Bust facing forward, wearing **_tiara with two pellet-in-crescents_**, diadem band below tiara; to left, Greek legend, ΦPA; to right, pellet in crescent above **_anchor with one or two crossbars_** at top; pellet border.

Rev: Artemis, sometimes radiate, standing right, holding bow in one hand, plucking arrow from her quiver with other hand; around her, Greek legend, ΦPAATHC BACIΛЄAC (*Phraates King*); pellet border.

Note: The legend on the reverse appears in a variety of configurations, and often has missing letters, letters in incorrect sequences, and corrupted letter forms. On later coins, the king's name is written as ΠPAATHC.

Æ Drachms

Subtype 1-1A   **Obv:** two crossbars on anchor.
Rev: BACIΛЄAC on the left; ΦPAATHC on the right, both reading inside-out.

a.

b.

c.

Subtype 1-1B   **Obv:** two crossbars on anchor.
Rev: ΦPAATHC on the left; BACIΛЄAC on the right, both reading outside-in.

a.

b.

c.

Subtype 1-1C Obv: two crossbars on anchor.
Rev: ΒΑCΙΛЄΑC on the left, reading outside-in; ΠΡΑΑΤΗC on the right, inside-out.
Note: the legends on this type are usually corrupted.

a.

b.

Subtype 1-2A Obv: one crossbar on anchor.
Rev: ΒΑCΙΛ[...] on the left; ΦΡΔΔΤΗC on the right, both reading inside-out.

a.

b.

Subtype 1-2B Obv: one crossbar on anchor.
Rev: ΦΡΑΑΤΗC on the left; ΒΑCΙΛЄΑ on the right, both reading outside-in.

a.

Subtype 1-2C **Obv:** one crossbar on anchor.
Rev: ΒΑCΙΛЄΑC on the left; ΠΡΑΑΤΗC on the right, both retrograde, reading outside-in.

a.

b.

Type 14.2
Obv: Bust facing forward, wearing *tiara with two pellet-in-crescents* and dotted rim, one or two diadem bands below tiara; to right, pellet in crescent above *anchor with one or two crossbars* at top; sometimes a pellet between the bust and anchor; pellet border.
Rev: Eagle standing left, *sometimes with head right*, wings spread, *talons facing downward or forward*; *sometimes crescents in fields*; pellet border.
Note: There is great variation in the style of bust and eagle.

Æ Drachms

Subtype 1-1 **Obv:** two crossbars on anchor.
Rev: talons downward.

a.

Subtype 1-2A **Obv:** one crossbar on anchor.
Rev: talons downward.

a.

b.

c.

120   PHRAATES

d.

e.

f.

g.

h.

i.

Subtype 1-2B   Obv: one crossbar on anchor; crude engraving.
Rev: talons downward; crude engraving.
Note: certain details, such as the tiara, are lacking on the obverse image. Perhaps an imitative issue?

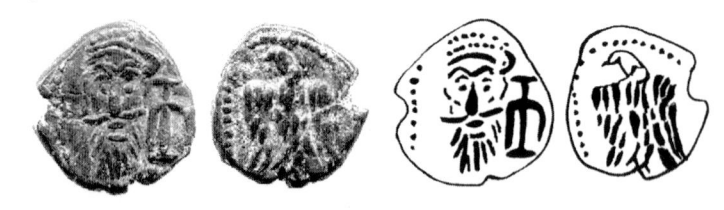

a.

Subtype 1-2C   Obv: one crossbar on anchor; pellet between bust and anchor.
Rev: talons downward.

a.

Subtype 1-3 Obv: one crossbar on anchor.
Rev: talons forward.

a.

Subtype 1-4A Obv: one crossbar on anchor.
Rev: talons downward; crescents flanking, facing outward.

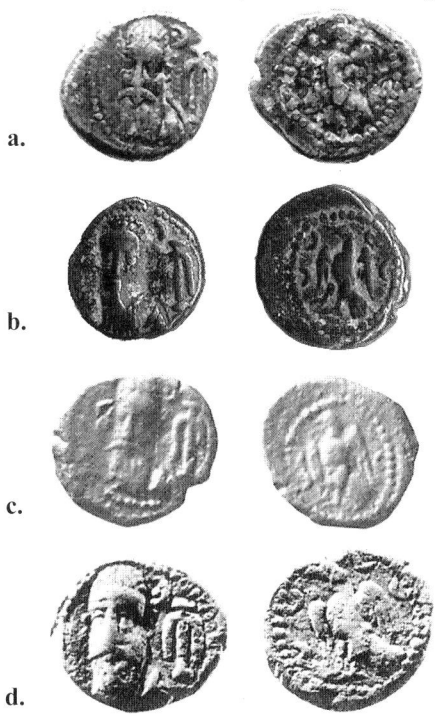

a.

b.

c.

d.

Subtype 1-4B Obv: one crossbar on anchor.
Rev: talons downward; crescents flanking, facing inwards.

a.

Subtype 1-5 Obv: one crossbar on anchor.
Rev: eagle's head right; talons downward.

a.

b.

Type 14.3

Obv: Bust facing forward, wearing *tiara with two pellet-in-crescents* and dotted rim, one or two diadem bands below tiara; to right, pellet in crescent above *anchor with one crossbar* at top; sometimes a pellet between the bust and anchor; pellet border.
Rev: Eagle standing left or right, wings closed, holding in its beak a diadem; pellet border.

Æ Drachms

Subtype 1-1   **Rev:** eagle standing left.

a.

b.

c.

Subtype 1-2   **Rev:** eagle standing right.

a.

Type 14.4

Obv: Bust facing forward, wearing *tiara with two pellet-in-crescents* and dotted rim, one or two diadem bands below tiara; to right, pellet in crescent above *anchor with one or two crossbars* at top; sometimes a pellet between the bust and anchor; pellet border.
Rev: Tied diadem with one or two bands, with or without fine lines between the bands; sometimes, to either side, pellet-in-crescents; pellet border.

Æ Drachms

Subtype 1-1A   **Rev:** plain diadem of two bands; pellet-in-crescents facing upwards.

a.

b.

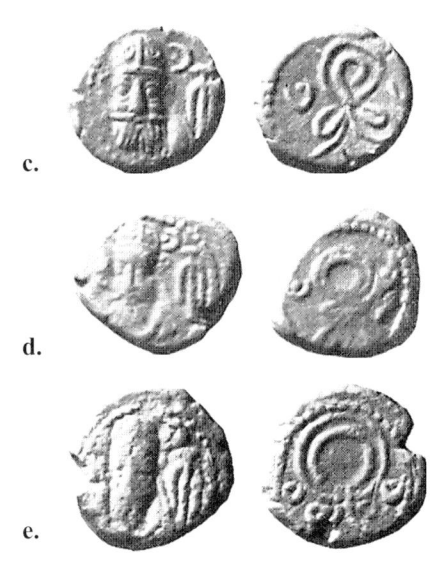

c.

d.

e.

Subtype 1-1B   **Rev:** plain diadem of two bands; pellet-in-crescents facing outward.

a.

Subtype 1-1C   **Rev:** plain diadem of two bands; no pellet-in-crescents.

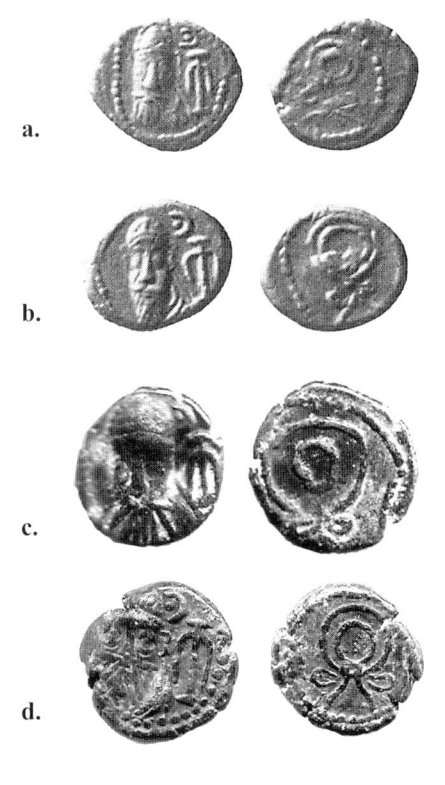

a.

b.

c.

d.

Subtype 1-2   **Rev:** diadem of two bands with fine lines; no pellet-in-crescents.

a.

b.

Subtype 1-3   **Rev:** diadem of one band; no pellet-in-crescents.

a.

Type 14.5

Obv: Bust facing forward, wearing *tiara with two pellet-in-crescents*, dotted rim, and diadem band below; to right, pellet in crescent above anchor with one crossbar at top; pellet border.
Rev: Crescents in regular or irregular pattern; no border.

Æ Drachms

Subtype 1-1   **Rev:** crescents in regular pattern.

a.

b.

c.

Note: on this and the following example, the crescents radiate outward in a cross-like pattern. On the former, another crescent is in each quarter formed by the cross pattern.

d.

Subtype 1-2   Rev: crescents in irregular pattern.

a.

b.

Type 14.6

Obv: Bust facing left, wearing ***tiara with pellet-in-crescent*** and dotted rim, diadem band below tiara; to left, Greek legend, ΦΡΑ; to right, pellet in crescent above ***anchor with one crossbar*** at top; pellet border.
Rev: Artemis, sometimes radiate, standing right, holding bow in one hand, plucking arrow from her quiver with other hand; around her, Greek legend, BACIΛЄVC ΦΡΑΑΤΗC (*Phraates King*); pellet border.
Note: The reverse legend appears in many configurations, often with missing letters, misspellings, and blundered letters. On later coins, the king's name is written as ΠΡΑΑΤΗC.

Æ Drachms

Subtype 1-1   Rev: Artemis not radiate; BAC[...] on the left; ΦΡΑ[...] on the right, retrograde; both reading inside-out.

a.

Note: this is the only example known of this early issue.

Subtype 1-2   Rev: Artemis radiate; BACIΛЄVC on the left, reading outside-in; ΠΡΑΑΤΗC on the right, reading inside-out; both retrograde.

a.

b.

Subtype 1-3 **Rev:** Artemis not radiate; ΒΑCΙΛЄVC on the left, reading outside-in; ΠΡΑΑΤΗC on the right, reading inside-out; both retrograde.

a.

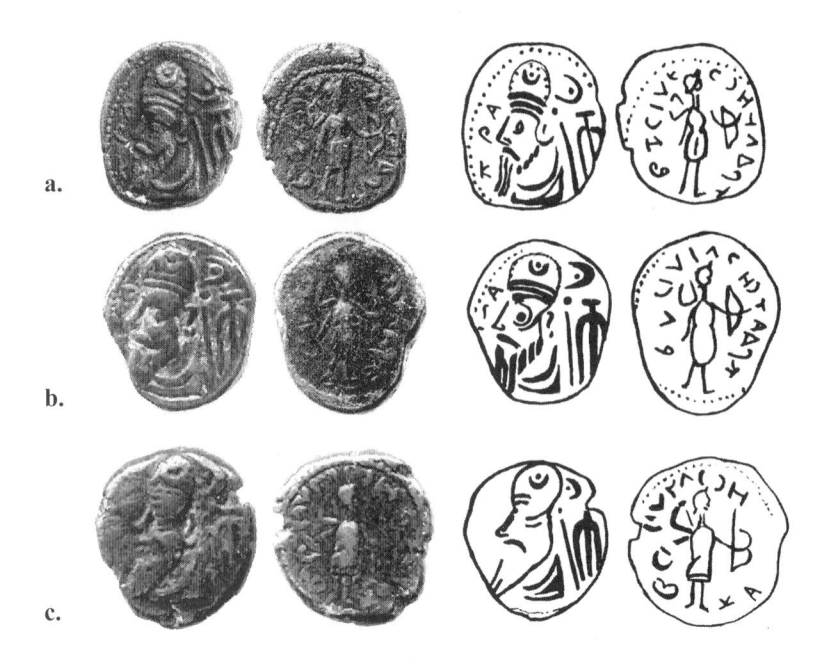

b.

c.

Type 14.7

Obv: Bust facing left, wearing *tiara with pellet-in-crescent*, diadem bands below tiara; to left, Aramaic legend in *one or two* lines [tetradrachms only]; to right, *star or pellet* in crescent above *anchor with one or two crossbars* at top; pellet border.
Rev: Dashes or crescents in regular or irregular pattern; no border.
Note: The Aramaic legends on the tetradrachms generally appear as such:

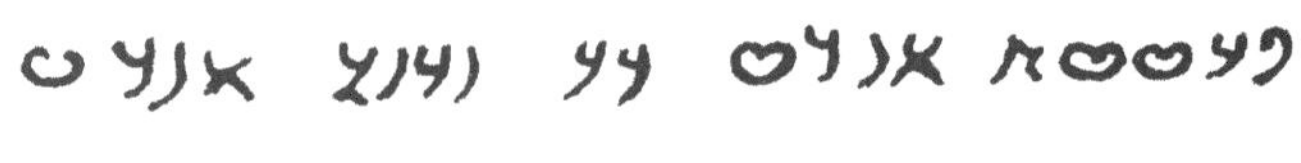 ꜥꜣꜣꜣ ꜣꜣꜣ ꜣꜣ ꜣꜣꜣꜣ ꜣꜣꜣꜣꜣ	**pr"t MLK' BR wrwd MLK'** *King Phraates, Son of King Orodes*
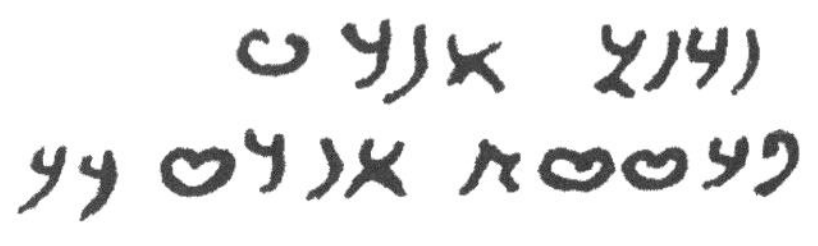 ꜣꜣꜣꜣꜣ ꜣꜣꜣꜣ ꜣꜣ ꜣꜣꜣꜣ ꜣꜣꜣꜣꜣ	**pr"t MLK'** *King Phraates* **BR wrwd MLK'** *Son of King Orodes*

Æ Tetradrachms

Subtype 1-1A **Obv:** two crossbars on anchor; star in crescent; 1-line legend.
Rev: dashes in regular, parallel pattern.

a.

Subtype 1-1B **Obv:** two crossbars on anchor; star in crescent; 2-line legend.
Rev: dashes in regular, parallel pattern.

a.

Note: The reverse of this example is very poorly preserved, and is not representative of the type.

Subtype 1-2 **Obv:** one crossbar on anchor; pellet in crescent; 2-line legend.
Rev: dashes in regular, parallel pattern.

a.

Æ Drachms

Subtype 2-1 **Obv:** small, narrow bust; one crossbar on anchor; pellet in crescent.
Rev: Dashes in regular, parallel or perpendicular pattern.

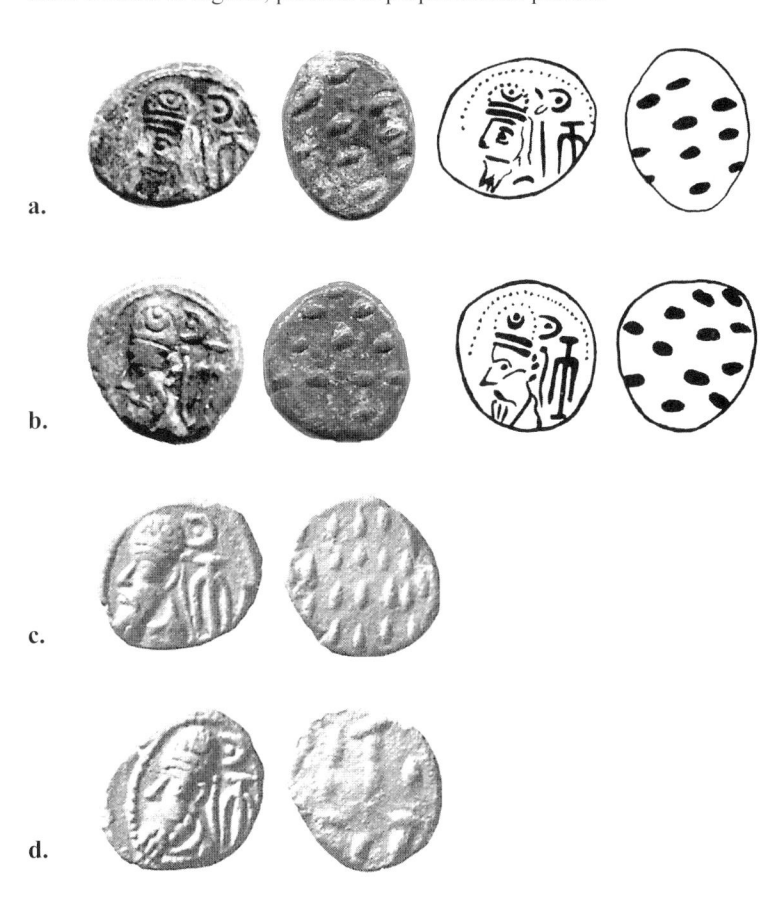

a.

b.

c.

d.

Subtype 2-2A Obv: Small, narrow bust; one crossbar on anchor; pellet in crescent.
Rev: Dashes in parallel lines of V-shaped patterns.

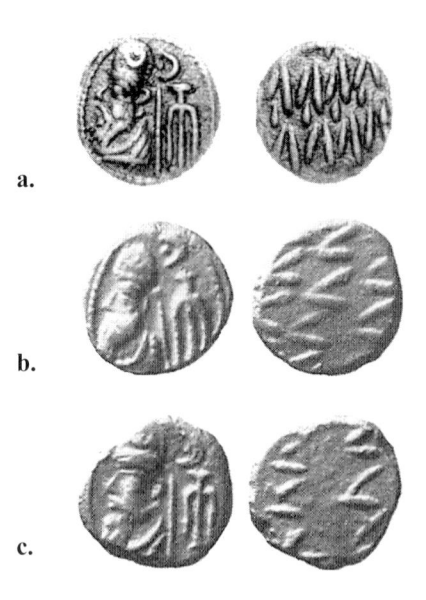

a.

b.

c.

Subtype 2-2B Obv: Large, broad bust; one crossbar on anchor; pellet in crescent.
Rev: Dashes in parallel lines of V-shaped patterns.

a.

b.

Subtype 2-3 Obv: Small, narrow bust; one crossbar on anchor; pellet in crescent.
Rev: Crescents in regular or irregular pattern.

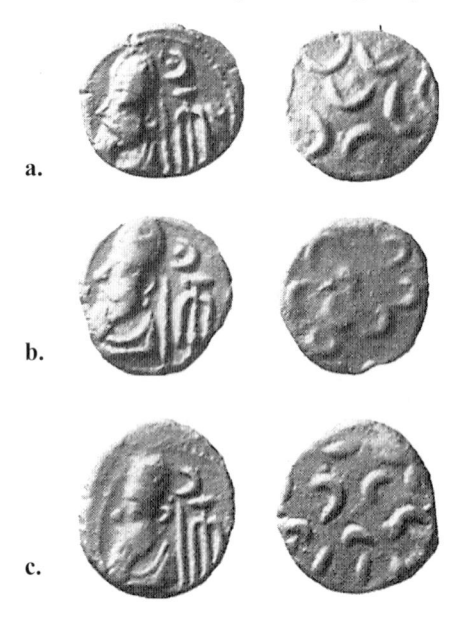

a.

b.

c.

d.

Type 14.8

Obv: Bust facing left, wearing ***tiara with pellet-in-crescent*** and dotted rim, four diadem bands below tiara; to left, Aramaic legend in two lines; to right, ***star*** in crescent above ***anchor with two crossbars*** at top; pellet above anchor; pellet border.

Rev: Degraded diademed, bearded head left; degraded legend around; no border.

Note: This type is represented by two coins that recently appeared on the market. They have been catalogued variously as Orodes I and Phraates. Based on the tiara type, I have placed them under Phraates. The curious aspects of the coins are the absence of a legend on the obverse, the dress of the king that is similar to Late Kamnaskirid kings (Types 8-9), the style of the star in the crescent, and the reverse which has the characteristics of the early Elymais Arsacid dynasty coins (Type 10) with the bust within four lines of legend.

Æ Tetradrachms

Subtype 1-1   No variation.

a.

b.

OSROES
(1st quarter of 2nd century AD)

Type 15.1
Obv: Bust left, with long beard, and hair dressed in Parthian fashion, with a large tuft behind the face extending to the back of the head, topped by a large tuft bound with a diadem, its ties streaming behind; pellet border.
Rev: Artemis standing right, head left, holding bow in right hand; degraded Greek legend in irregular frame around; no border.
Note: Petrowicz read the legend, with doubt, as ΒΑΙΛΕΥΖ ΧΟΣΡΟΙ.

Æ Drachms

Subtype 1-1   No variation.

a.

Type 15.2
Obv: Bust left, with long beard, and hair dressed in Parthian fashion, with a large tuft behind the face extending to the back of the head, topped by a large tuft bound with a diadem, its ties streaming behind; pellet border.
Rev: Artemis standing right, holding bow in left hand, right hand drawing bow from quiver on her back; legend in irregular frame around; no border.

Æ Drachms

Subtype 1-1   No variation.

a.

Type 15.3
Obv: Bust left, with long beard, and hair dressed in Parthian fashion, with a large tuft behind the face extending to the back of the head, topped by a large tuft bound with a diadem, its ties streaming behind; pellet border.
Rev: Diademed female bust right; no border.

Æ Obols

Subtype 1-1   No variation.

a.

ORODES III
(2nd century AD)

Type 16.1
Obv: Bust facing left, wearing *tiara with anchor* and dotted rim, diadem band below tiara, ribbon falling behind bust from dot; to right, pellet in crescent above *anchor with one crossbar* at top; with or without pellet border.
Rev: Bust of Artemis right, wearing calathus, sometimes radiate; around her, Greek legend, BACIΛEYK YPωΔHC (*King Orodes*); pellet border.
Notes: The bust of Orodes on this type exhibits a relatively refined or crude style. Also, the legend is typically corrupted, usually with letters missing and malformed.

Æ Drachms

Subtype 1-1   Obv: refined style; pellet border.
Rev: YPωΔHC on the left, reading inside-out, BACIΛEYK on the right, reading outside-in.

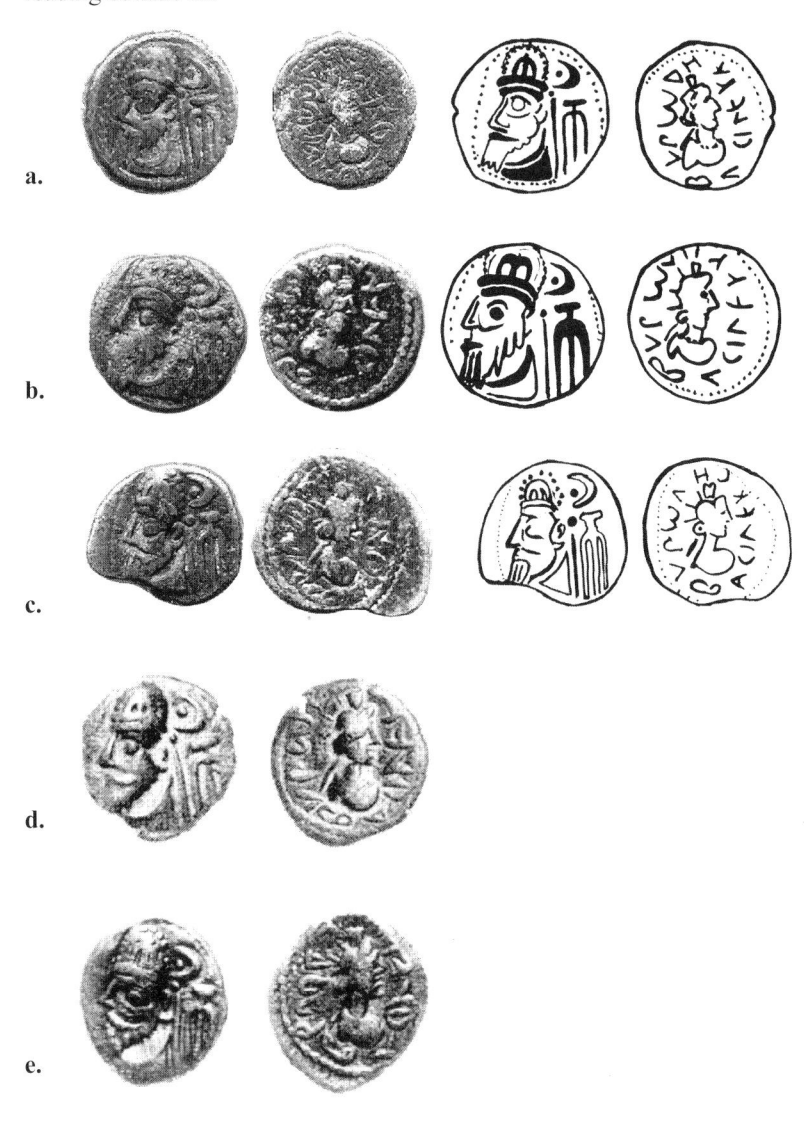

a.

b.

c.

d.

e.

ORODES III

Subtype 1-2 Obv: crude style; no border.
Rev: YPωΔHC on the left, reading inside-out, BACIΛEYK on the right, reading outside-in.

a.

b.

Subtype 1-3A Obv: refined style; pellet border.
Rev: retrograde legends - BACIΛEYK on the left, reading outside-in, YPωΔHC on the right, reading inside-out.

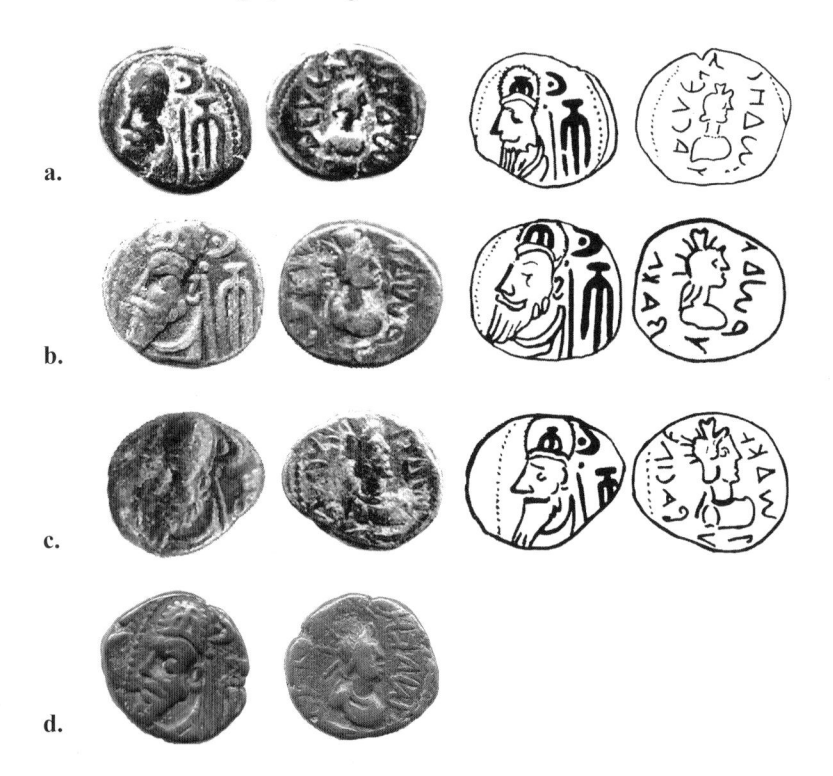

a.

b.

c.

d.

Subtype 1-3B Obv: refined style; pellet border.
Rev: retrograde legends - BACIΛEYK on the left, reading outside-in, YPωΔHC on the right, reading outside-in.

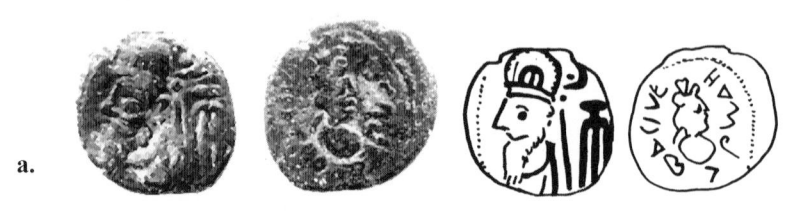

a.

Type 16.2

Obv: Bust facing left, wearing *tiara with anchor* and dotted rim, diadem band below tiara, usually with ribbon falling behind bust from dot; to right, pellet in crescent above *anchor with one or two crossbars* at top; sometimes a star between bust and anchor; pellet border.

Rev: Bust of Belos left, right, or facing forward, usually with bead necklace and earrings; cornucopia behind; pellet border.

Æ Drachms

Subtype 1-1   **Obv:** diadem with ribbon and dot; one crossbar on anchor.
  Rev: Belos right.

a.

b.

c.

Subtype 1-2A   **Obv:** diadem with ribbon and dot; one crossbar on anchor.
  Rev: Belos left.

a.

b.

Note: this example has a star between the bust and anchor.

c.

d.

ORODES III

Subtype 1-2B Obv: diadem dot (ribbon tie) only; one crossbar on anchor.
Rev: Belos left.

a.

b.

Subtype 1-2C Obv: diadem without dot or ribbon; one crossbar on anchor.
Rev: Belos left.

a.

b.

Subtype 1-3 Obv: diadem with ribbon and dot; two crossbars on anchor.
Rev: Belos left.

a.

Subtype 1-4 Obv: diadem with ribbon and dot; two crossbars on anchor.
Rev: Belos facing forward.

a.

b.

Type 16.3

Obv: Bust facing left, wearing *tiara with anchor* and dotted rim, diadem band below tiara, usually with ribbon falling behind bust from dot; to left on tetradrachms, Aramaic legend; to right, pellet in crescent above *anchor with one or two crossbars* at top; sometimes a star or pellet between bust and anchor; pellet border.
Rev: Anchor in field of dashes or other symbols; no border.
Note: The tetradrachms of this type are obverse die linked to the tetradrachms of Type 16.4. The legend on the tetradrachms generally appears as such:

ꟃꟃꟃ ꟃꟃꟃ	wrwd MLK' *King Orodes*

Also, the bust on the drachms is slender or broad, the latter covering more than half the field.

Æ Tetradrachms

Subtype 1-1   **Obv:** two crossbars on anchor; star between bust and anchor.
              Rev: anchor in field of regular, parallel dashes.

a.

Subtype 1-2   **Obv:** one crossbar on anchor; star between bust and anchor.
              Rev: anchor in field of regular, parallel dashes.

a.

Æ Drachms

Subtype 2-1A   **Obv:** slender bust; one crossbar on anchor.
               Rev: anchor in field of regular, parallel dashes.

a.

b.

c.

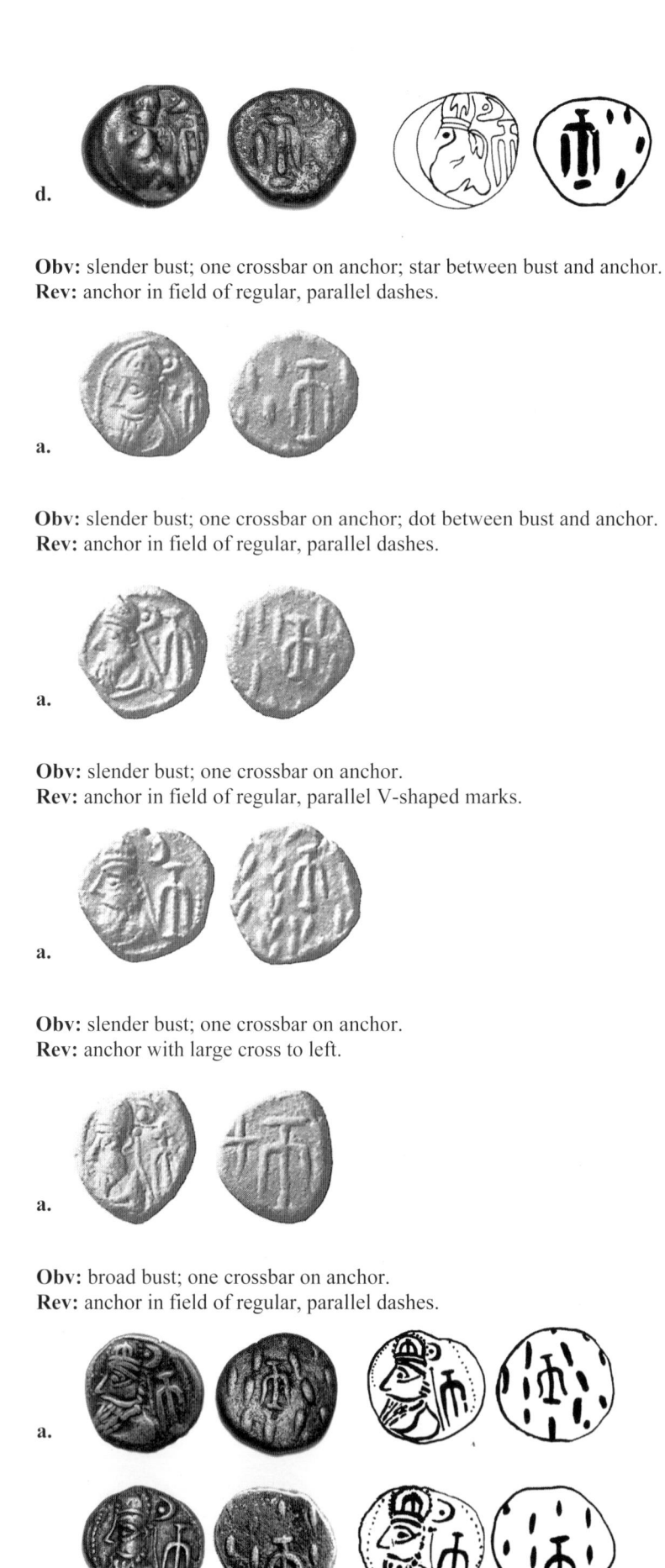

d.

Subtype 2-1B **Obv:** slender bust; one crossbar on anchor; star between bust and anchor.
Rev: anchor in field of regular, parallel dashes.

a.

Subtype 2-1C **Obv:** slender bust; one crossbar on anchor; dot between bust and anchor.
Rev: anchor in field of regular, parallel dashes.

a.

Subtype 2-1D **Obv:** slender bust; one crossbar on anchor.
Rev: anchor in field of regular, parallel V-shaped marks.

a.

Subtype 2-1E **Obv:** slender bust; one crossbar on anchor.
Rev: anchor with large cross to left.

a.

Subtype 2-2A **Obv:** broad bust; one crossbar on anchor.
Rev: anchor in field of regular, parallel dashes.

a.

b.

c.

Subtype 2-2B   Obv: broad bust; one crossbar on anchor.
Rev: anchor with small symbol to right, in field of regular, parallel crosses.

a.

b.

Subtype 2-2C   Obv: broad bust; one crossbar on anchor.
Rev: anchor in field of crosses and dots in irregular pattern.

a.

Type 16.4

Obv: Bust facing left, wearing *tiara with anchor* and dotted rim, diadem band below tiara, usually with ribbon falling behind bust from dot; to left on tetradrachms, Aramaic legend; to right, pellet in crescent above *anchor with one or two crossbars* at top; sometimes a star or pellet between bust and anchor; pellet border.
Rev: Field of dashes in regular or irregular pattern; no border.
Note: The tetradrachms of this type are obverse die linked to the tetradrachms of Type 16.3. The legend on the tetradrachms generally appears as such:

ⵙⵢⵉⵀ ⵢⵢⵢ	wrwd MLK'
	King Orodes

On the drachms, the bust can be relatively slender or broad, with the latter covering more than half of the field. Both are somewhat crude in style, but the broad variety are exceptionally so. Also, the reverse types appear to correlate to the respective bust type.

Æ Tetradrachms

Subtype 1-1   Obv: one crossbar on anchor; star between bust and anchor.
Rev: field of regular, parallel dashes.

a.

ORODES III

Subtype 1-2 **Obv:** two crossbars on anchor; star between bust and anchor.
Rev: field of regular, parallel dashes.

a.

Æ Drachms

Subtype 2-1A **Obv:** slender bust of better style; one crossbar on anchor.
Rev: field of regular, parallel dashes.

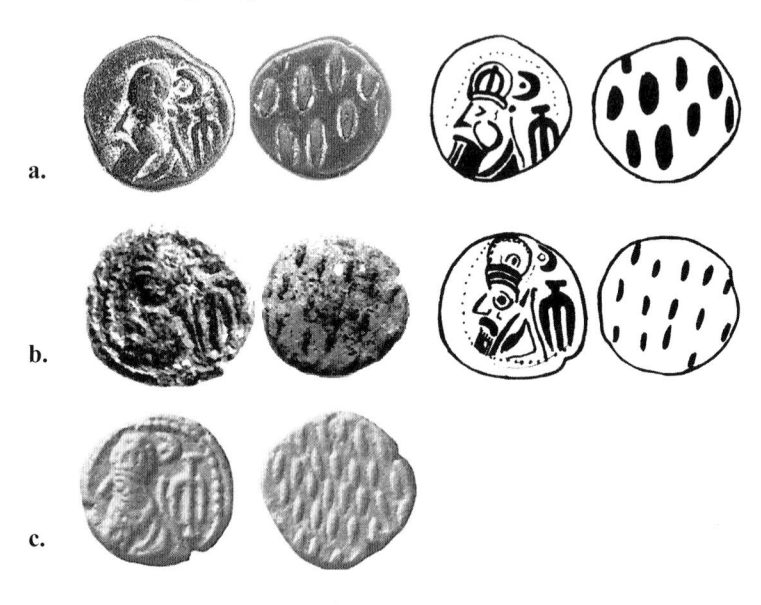

a.

b.

c.

Subtype 2-1B **Obv:** slender bust of better style; one crossbar on anchor.
Rev: field of regular, parallel V-shaped marks.

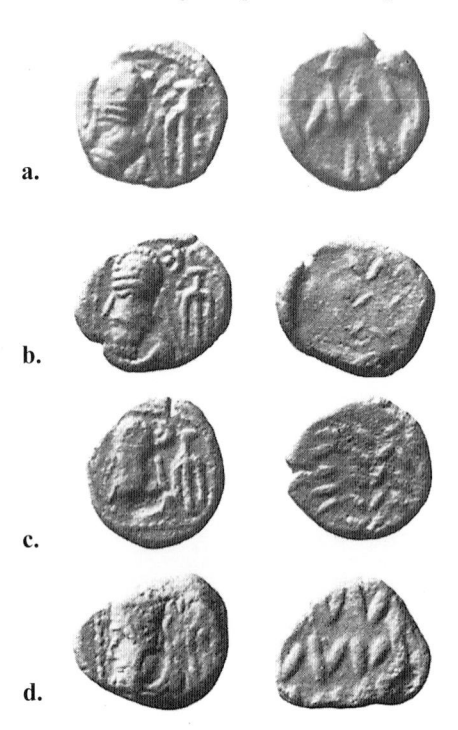

a.

b.

c.

d.

Subtype 2-2 **Obv:** broad bust of poor style; one crossbar on anchor.
Rev: field of dashes in irregular pattern.

a.

b.

ORODES IV
(Circa 2nd half of 2nd century AD)

Type 17.1
Obv: Bust facing left, wearing broad diadem band, with large hair tuft on top of and on side of head, flowing backward; to left, Aramaic legend or anchor; pellet border.
Rev: Bust of female left, hair tied above, with long braid falling behind; to left, Aramaic legend; pellet border.
Note: The legends are typically corrupted or incomplete, but generally should appear as such:

Obverse	ⵔⵓⵊⵅ ⵟ⵿ⵢⵎ	**wrwd MLK'** *King Orodes*
Reverse	ⵎⵟ⵿ⵙⵉ	**wlp'n** *Ulfan*

Æ Drachms

    Subtype 1-1   **Obv:** legend to left.

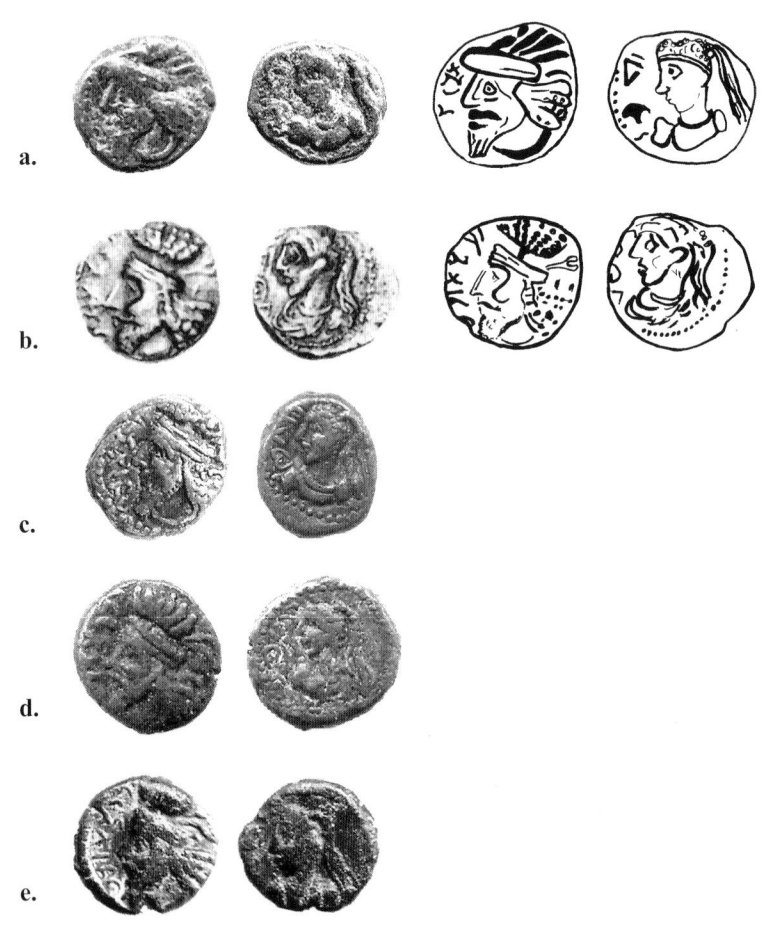

a.

b.

c.

d.

e.

Note: This example has a full legend on the obverse.

    Subtype 1-2   **Obv:** Anchor to left.

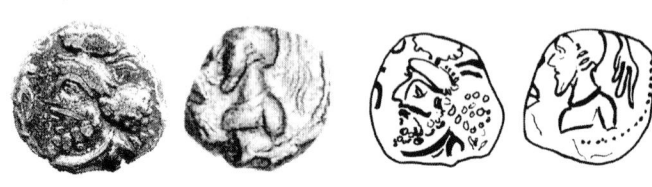

a.

b.

c.

Type 17.2
Obv: Bust facing forward, or slightly left, wearing diadem band, with large hair tuft on the top and sides of head; pellet border.
Rev: Bust of Artemis left, wearing low tiara with crest of dots; to right, anchor with one or two crossbars on top; pellet border.

Æ Drachms

Subtype 1-1   Rev: anchor with one crossbar.

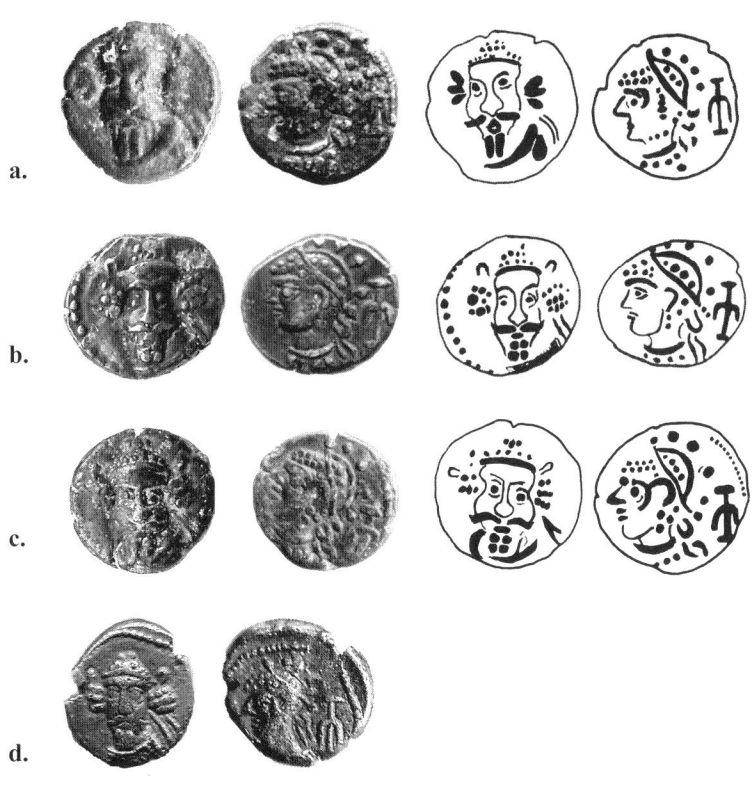

a.

b.

c.

d.

Subtype 1-2   Rev: anchor with two crossbars.

a.

Type 17.3

Obv: Bust facing forward, or slightly left, wearing diadem band, with large hair tufts on the sides of head, top hair as pellets, sometimes with small tuft; pellet border.
Rev: Anchor with pellet-in-crescent to either side; all within wreath or crossed cornucopias; no border.

Æ Drachms

Subtype 1-1   Rev: type within wreath.

a.

Subtype 1-2A   Rev: type within upward crossed cornucopias.

a.

b.

Subtype 1-2B   Rev: type within downward crossed cornucopias.

a.

b.

ORODES V
(Late 2nd - early 3rd centuries AD)

Type 18.1

Obv: Bust facing left, diademed, with hair tuft on top of head; sometimes to left, Aramaic legend; sometimes to right, anchor; pellet border.
Rev: Bust of Artemis left, wearing low tiara with crest of dots; sometimes to right, anchor; pellet border.
Note: The legends are typically corrupted or incomplete, but generally should appear as such:

ⲤⳞΛⵝ Ɣ)Ɣ)	wrwd MLK' *King Orodes*

Æ Drachms

Subtype 1-1A   Obv: legend to left; no anchor.
Rev: anchor to right.

a.

b.

c.

Subtype 1-1B   Obv: legend to left; anchor to right.
Rev: no anchor.

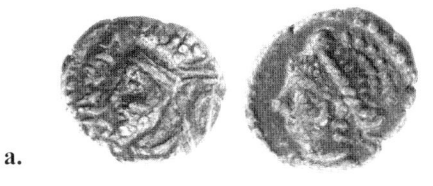

a.

Subtype 1-2A   Obv: no legend; no anchor.
Rev: no anchor.

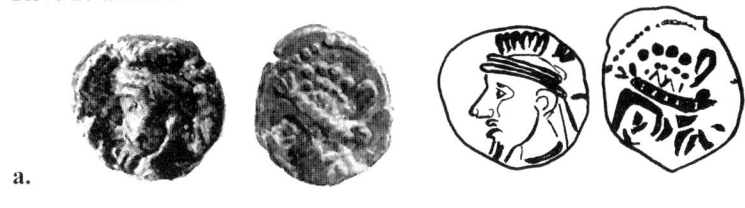

a.

ORODES V

b.

c.

d.

Subtype 1-2B **Obv:** no legend, no anchor.
Rev: anchor to right.

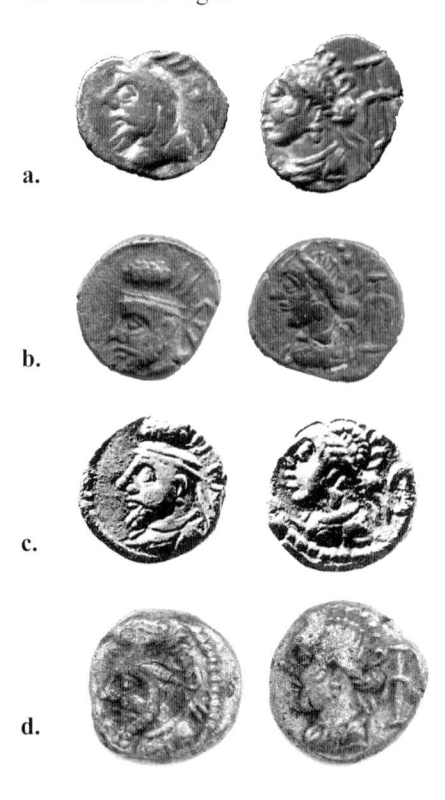

a.

b.

c.

d.

Subtype 1-2C **Obv:** no legend, anchor to right.
Rev: no anchor.

a.

PRINCE A
(Late 2nd - early 3rd centuries AD)

Type 19.1

Obv: Bust facing left, wearing diadem of one or two bands, usually with row of dots above, side whiskers of one or two rows of dots, usually a hair tuft at back of head; sometimes above, star or dot in crescent; sometimes to right, anchor with one or two crossbars; pellet border.

Rev: Artemis standing right, holding bow in one hand, plucking arrow from her quiver with other hand; sometimes with crescent to left, one or two dots or dashes to right; pellet border.

Notes: The varieties with hair tuft are always accompanied by the star or dot in crescent above the head and anchor to the right. These symbols, however, are often struck off the flan. Also, the varieties with whiskers as a double-row of dots is the only variety on which the crescent appears on the reverse.

Æ Drachms

Subtype 1-1A — **Obv:** Hair tuft at back of head; whiskers as double row of dots; star or dot in crescent above; anchor to right.

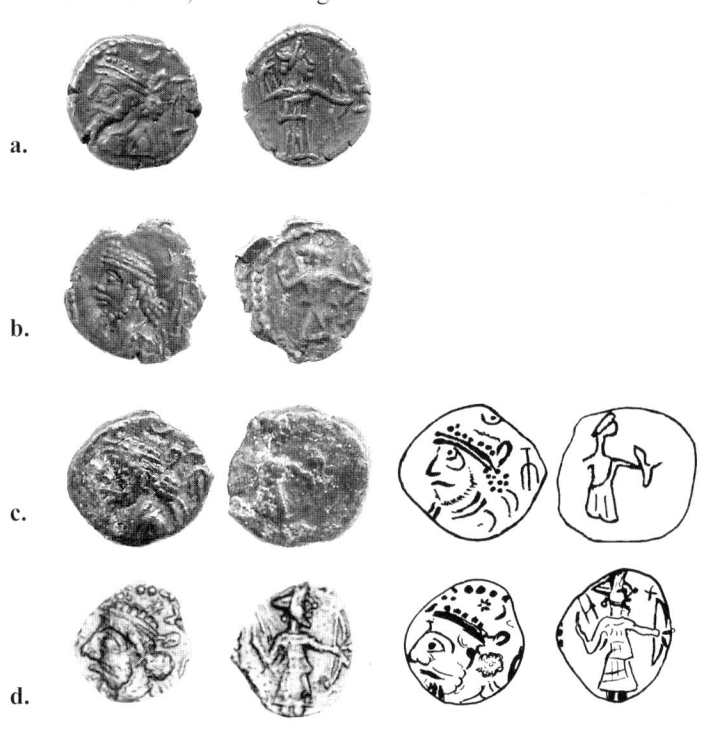

a.

b.

c.

d.

Note: the cross-like object in the right field of the reverse may not be an intentional mark.

e.

Note: this and the following three examples have a crescent to the left on the reverse.

f.

146 PRINCE A

g.

h.

i.

Note: while this example belongs in this subtype, the style is very different: a much larger bust, and more refined Artemis.

Subtype 1-1B   **Obv:** Hair tuft at back of head; whiskers as single row of dots; star or dot in crescent above; anchor to right.

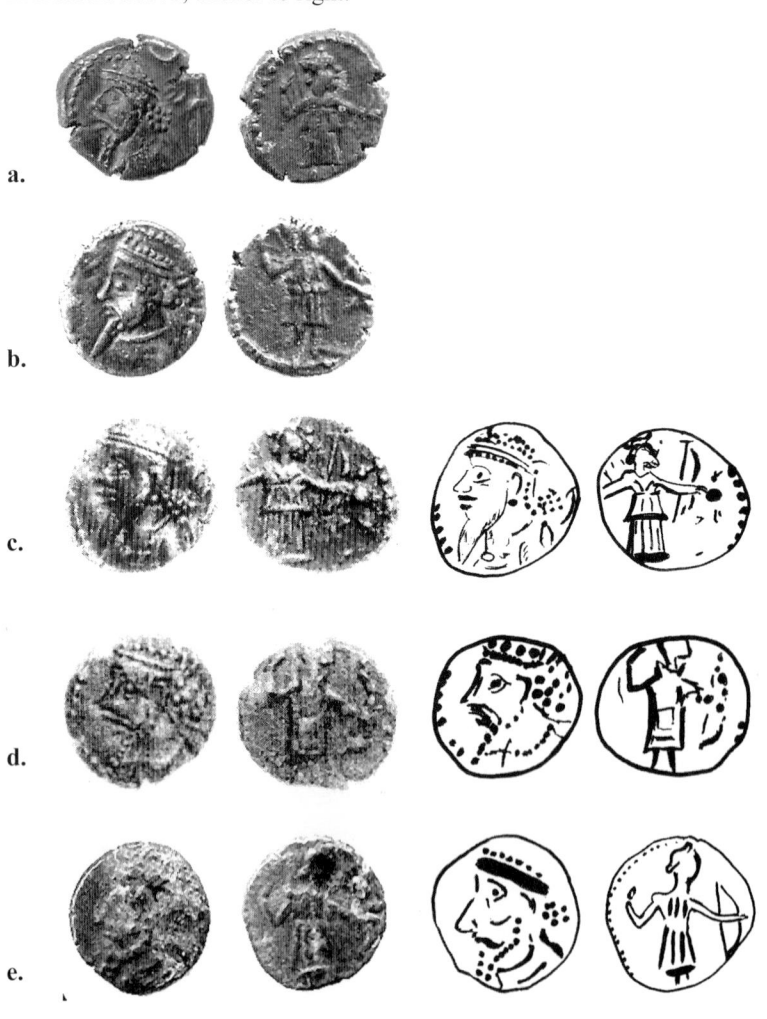

a.

b.

c.

d.

e.

d.

Subtype 1-2   **Obv:** No hair tuft at back of head; whiskers as single row of dots; no star or dot in crescent above, nor anchor to right.

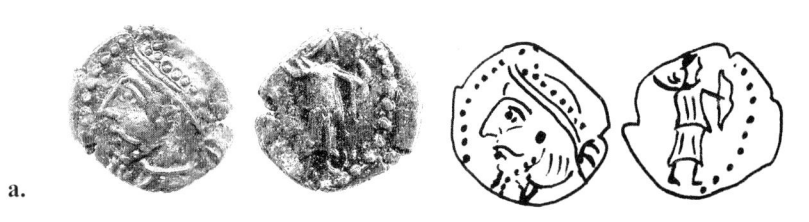

a.

PRINCE B
(3rd century AD)

Type 20.1

Obv: Bust facing left, wearing diadem of two bands, hair tuft on top of head tied with ribbon, its ends flowing behind, another hair tuft at back of head; sometimes to right, pellet-in-crescent above anchor; pellet border.
Rev: Athena standing right, left, or facing forward, holding spear in one hand, and shield in the other; pellet border.
Note: The pellet-in-crescent and anchor are often off the flan. Also, Athena's head is sometimes facing the opposite direction.

Æ Drachms

Subtype 1-1A   **Obv:** to right, anchor with pellet-in-crescent above.
                     Rev: Athena standing right, spear in right hand, shield in left.

a.

b.

Subtype 1-1B   **Obv:** to right, anchor with pellet-in-crescent above.
                     Rev: Athena standing facing forward, head left, spear in right hand, shield in left.

a.

b.

Subtype 1-2   **Obv:** no anchor with pellet-in-crescent above.
                     Rev: Athena standing left, shield in right hand, spear in left.

a.

Æ Hemidrachms

Subtype 2-1   Rev: Athena standing facing forward, head left, spear in right hand, shield in left.

a.

Note: the obverse on the only example of this coin is just off center enough to make the presence of the anchor and pellet-in-crescent uncertain.

UNIDENTIFIED KING
(Uncertain dates)

Type 21.1
Obv: Bust facing left, details unclear.
Rev: Anchor with one or two crossbars at top, all within wreath.
Note: Too few of these coins are known to determine their denomination.

Æ Units

Subtype 1-1   **Rev:** One crossbar on anchor.

a.

b.

Subtype 1-2   **Rev:** Two crossbars on anchor.

a.

Type 21.2
Obv: Bust facing right, details unclear.
Rev: Upturned crescent with three dots below, all within wreath.
Note: Too few of these coins are known to determine their denomination.

Æ Units

Subtype 1-1   No variation.

a.

Appendix 1 – Concordances

The following is a listing of concordances to the standard references that are typically used to catalogue Elymaean coins.

Please note that the numbers listed are general concordances to the particular denomination of each type, and do not include specific varieties (subtypes). Each reference should be consulted for citation to the correct variety.

Type #	De Morgan	BMC	Sear	Alram
1.1.1	-	-	-	429
1.2.1	-	-	-	430
1A.1.1	-	-	-	-
2.1.1	1	Pl. LIII, 6	6169	431
2.1.2	-	-	-	432, 433
2.2.1	-	-	-	-
2.3.1	-	-	-	440, 441
2.4.1	-	-	-	434
2.5.1	-	-	-	435
2.6.1	-	-	-	436
2.7.1	-	-	-	438
2.8.1	-	-	-	444
2.9.1	-	-	-	443
2.10.1	-	-	-	437
2.11.1	-	-	-	439
3.1.1	-	-	-	445
3.2.1	-	-	-	446
4.1.1[1]	2	-	6170	-
4.2.1[2]	-	-	-	-
4.3.1[3]	-	-	-	-
4.4.1[4]	-	-	-	-
4.5.1[5]	-	-	-	-
5.1.1	-	-	-	447
5.2.1	-	-	-	450
5.3.1	-	-	-	453
5.4.1	-	-	-	451
5.5.1	-	-	-	448
5.6.1	-	-	-	449
5.7.1	-	-	-	452
6.1.1	-	-	-	-
7.1.1	4	Pl. XXXVIII, 1-3	6171	454
7.1.2	5	Pl. XXXVIII, 4	6172	455
7.1.3	6	-	6173	456
7.1.4	7	-	6174	457
8.1.1	-	-	-	-
8.1.2	-	Pl. XXXVIII, 5	6176	-
8.1.3	-	-	-	-
8.2.1	3	-	6175	458
8.2.2	-	Pl. XXXVIII, 6	6176	459
8.2.3	-	-	-	460

[1] Sellwood 14.1, 14.2 (Parthia).
[2] Sellwood 14.4 (Parthia).
[3] Sellwood 14.3 (Parthia).
[4] Sellwood 14.6 (Parthia).
[5] Sellwood 14.5 (Parthia).

APPENDIX 1 - CONCORDANCES

8.3.1	-	-	-	461
8.3.2	-	-	-	462
8.3.3	-	-	-	-
9.1.1	8, 10, 14-16	Pl. XXXVIII, 8	5884	463
9.1.2	9, 11	Pl. XXXVIII, 9-10	5885	464
9.1.3	12	Pl. XXXVIII, 11-12	5886	465
9.1.4	13	Pl. XXXVIII, 13-14	5887	466
9.1.5	-	-	-	-
9.2.1	-	-	-	-
10.1.1	17 var. (Pl. II, 2)[6]	-	-	-
10.1.2	-	-	-	-
10.2.1	-	-	-	-
10.3.1	17	Pl. XXXIX, 3-5	5888	NB1
10.3.2	-	-		-
10.4.1	-	-		-
10.4.2	-	-		-
10.5.1	-	Pl. XXXIX, 5		-
10.5.2	-	-		-
10.6.1	-	Pg. 250, 18	5889	-
10.7.1	18	Pl. XXXIX, 6-10	5890	NB2
11.1.1	-	-	-	NB3
11.1.2	-	Pl. XXXIX, 6-11	-	-
12.1.1	47	Pl. XL, 20-24 Pl. LIII, 15	5906	479-481
12.2.1	48	Pl. XLI, 1	5907	482-484
12.3.1	50	Pl. XLI, 4-9	5910	-
12.4.1	51	Pl. LIII, 16	-	486
13.1.1	49	Pl. XLI, 2	5908-5909	485
13.2.1	44-45	Pl. XL, 10	5904	478
13.3.1	42	Pl. XL, 8-9	5903	477
13.3.2	46	Pl. XL, 13	5905	-
14.1.1	33	Pl. XLI, 22	5898	474-476
14.2.1	37, 39	Pl. XLI, 24	5900	-
14.3.1	38	Pl. XLI, 25	-	-
14.4.1	40	Pl. XLI, 26-27	5901	-
14.5.1	-	Pl. XLI, 19	-	-
14.6.1	34-35	Pl. XLI, 10	5899	473
14.7.1	41	Pl. XLI, 16	5897	471-472
14.7.2	36.2-3	Pl. XLI, 17-21	-	-
14.8.1	-	-	-	-
15.1.1	22	-	-	487
15.2.1	22	-	-	487
15.3.1	-	-	-	-
16.1.1	23-24	Pl. XXXIX, 12-16	5892	469-470
16.2.1	25-26	Pl. XXXIX, 17-20 Pg. 257, 46-47	5893-5894	-
16.3.1	-	-	-	468
16.3.2	27	Pl. XL, 1-5	5895	-
16.4.1	32	Pl. LIII, 13	-	467
16.4.2	28	Pl. XL, 6-7	5896	-
17.1.1	52-53	Pl. XLII, 5-6	5912-5913	488-489
17.2.1	54	Pl. XLII, 2	5914	-
17.3.1	55	Pl. XLII, 1	5915	-

---

[6] De Morgan 17 specifies a star in crescent above the anchor, but the coin illustrated is a rosette without a crescent.

18.1.1	56-57	Pg. 282, 1, 6 Pl. XLII, 7-8	5916-5917	490
19.1.1	58-59	Pl. XLII, 13-18 Pg. 286, 18	5918-5919	-
20.1.1	60	Pl. XLII, 19-20 Pg. 287, 4-6	5920	-
21.1.1	-	-	-	-
21.2.1	-	Pl. XLII, 22-25	-	-

Appendix 2 – Sources, Die Links, Weight, and Size

The following is the list of source, weight and size for the coins illustrated in the catalogue. Die links between the coins are also noted.

4Δ = Tetradrachm; Δ = Drachm; 1/2 Δ = Hemidrachm; O = Obol; 1/2 O = Hemiobol; U = Unit; 1/2 U = Half Unit

	Sources & Die Links	**Denom. & Weight**[1]	**Size**[2]
Kamnaskires I Soter			
1.1.1-1a	Alram 429 = Le Rider 1969, 10 (obv. die link to 1.2.1-1a)	4Δ; 16.87	27
1.2.1-1a	Alram 430 = Le Rider 1969, 11 (obv. die link to 1.1.1-1a)	4Δ; 16.88	25
Kamnaskires I or II			
1A.1.1-1a	Le Rider 1965, pl. VIII, 85	4Δ; 14.20	27
Kamnaskires II Nikephores			
2.1.1-1a	Triton VII, 518	4Δ; 16.57	28
2.1.1-1b	Le Rider 1965, pl. VIII, D	4Δ; 16.63	28
2.1.1-2a	Le Rider 1965, pl. VIII, G	4Δ; 16.56	27
2.1.1-2b	Le Rider 1965, pl. VIII, H	4Δ; 16.65	29
2.1.1-3a	Peus 374, 124	4Δ; 15.57	29
2.1.1-4a	Private Collection	4Δ; 15.13	n/a
2.1.1-5a	CNG 66, 832	4Δ; 15.01	28
2.1.1-6a	CNG 55, 779	4Δ; 16.45	22
2.1.1-7a	CNG 75, 604	4Δ; 15.58	28
2.1.1-8a	CNG 72, 1010 = CNG 67, 994	4Δ; 16.17	26
2.1.2-1a	Album List 202, 231 = Kovacs XIII, 86 (obv. die link to 2.2.1-1b)	Δ; 4.13	18
2.1.2-1b	CNG E-Auction 122, 163 = Kovacs XV, 160 (obv. die link to 2.2.1-1a)	Δ; 3.82	19
2.1.2-2a	CNG Triton VII, 519	Δ; 4.03	18
2.1.2-3a	Alram 432 = Le Rider 1965, pl. LXXII, 9	Δ; n/a	17
2.1.2-4a	Alram 433 = Le Rider 1965, pl. LXXII, 10	Δ; n/a	17
2.2.1-1a	CNG Triton V, 1668 = Peus 368, 329	Δ; 3.90	20
2.3.1-1a	Le Rider 1965, pl. VIII, 92, 5	U; 2.12	15
2.3.1-1b	Alram 440 = Le Rider 1965, pl. IX, A	U; n/a	15
2.4.1-1a	Alram 434 = Le Rider 1965, pl. VIII, 86 ,1	U; 3.37	16
2.5.1-1a	Alram 435 = Le Rider 1965, pl. VIII, 87, 1	U; 3.35	15
2.6.1-1a	Alram 436 = Le Rider 1965, pl. IX, 88, 4	U; 3.47	15
2.7.1-1a	Le Rider 1965, pl. IX, 90, 9	U; 1.74	14
2.8.1-1a	Alram 444 = Le Rider 1965, pl. IX, 94	U; 2.17	15
2.9.1-1a	Le Rider 1965, pl. IX, 93, 8	1/2 U; 1.12	14
2.10.1-1a	Le Rider 1965, pl. IX, 89, 3	U; 2.81	15
2.11.1-1a	Alram 439 = Le Rider 1965, pl. IX, 91, 2	U; 3.03	15
Okkonapses			
3.1.1-1a	Alram 445 = MuM 66, 302 = Le Rider 1978, 1 (same dies as 3.1.1-1b)	4Δ; 16.39	27
3.1.1-1b	Auctiones 13, 421 (same dies as 3.1.1-1a)	4Δ; 16.65	30
3.2.1-1a	Le Rider 1965, pl. VI, 65, 2	U; 1.68	14

---

[1] Weight in grams.

[2] Size in millimeters, from 9 to 3 o'clock on obverse.

Phraates son of Mithradates I			
4.1.1-1a	Le Rider 1965, pl. X, A = De Morgan pl. 1, 2	4Δ; 16.30	26
4.1.1-2a	Le Rider 1965, pl. X, B	4Δ; 16.73	31
4.2.1-1a	Le Rider 1965, pl. X, 100, 15	U; 2.36	13
4.3.1-1a	Le Rider 1965, pl. X, 98, 11	U; 1.81	16
4.3.2-1a	Le Rider 1965, pl. X, 99, 1	1/2 U; 0.91	7
Tigraios			
5.1.1-1a	Peus 363, 5073	4Δ; 16.14	26
5.2.1-1a	Le Rider 1965, pl. X, 103, 9	U; 1.65	15
5.3.1-1a	Alram 453 = Le Rider 1965, pl. XI, 108, 3	U; 1.92	15
5.4.1-1a	Le Rider 1965, pl. X, 104, 4	U; 1.52	15
5.5.1-1a	Alram 448 = Le Rider 1965, pl. X, 101, 19	U; 2.13	15
5.6.1-1a	Alram 449 = Le Rider 1965, pl. LV, 102, 1	U; 2.17	16
5.7.1-1a	Alram 452 = Le Rider 1965, pl. X, 105, 1	U; 1.80	15
5.7.1-1b	Le Rider 1965, pl. XI, 106,2	U; 1.50	14
Dareios			
6.1.1-1a	Peus 368, 330	4Δ; 16.46	27
Kamnaskires III and Anzaze			
7.1.1-1a	Le Rider 1965, pl. LXXII, 11 = BMC 1, pl. XXXVIII, 1	4Δ; 15.69	27
7.1.1-2a	Peus 386, 359	4Δ; 15.02	28
7.1.1-3a	Leu 86, 448 = Peus 368, 331	4Δ; 16.35	27
7.1.1-4a	G&M 138, 157	4Δ; 13.62	28
7.1.1-5a	Leu 2, 301	4Δ; 16.08	26
7.1.1-6a	CNG Triton VII, 520	4Δ; 15.14	28
7.1.2-1Aa	Peus 392, 4393 = Peus 386, 360	Δ; 3.86	18
7.1.2-1Ba	Peus 374, 126 = Peus 368, 332	Δ; 3.70	17
7.1.2-2Aa	Le Rider 1965, pl. LXXII, 12 = Allotte de la Füye, *RN* 1902, pl. V, 5	Δ; n/a	18
7.1.2-2Ba	CNG Triton VII, 521	Δ; 3.94	17
7.1.2-3a	CNG E-Auction 102, 60	Δ; 3.45	17
7.1.2-4a	GM 101, 406 (same dies as 7.1.2-4b)	Δ; 3.89	16
7.1.2-4b	G&M 134, 1589 = G&M 129, 192 (same dies as 7.1.2-4a)	Δ; 3.91	16
7.1.2-5a	CNG E-Auction 122, 164	Δ; 3.68	18
7.1.3-1a	Peus 338, 54 = Peus 337, 174	1/2 Δ; 1.99	12
7.1.3-2a	G&M 138, 1524 = Peus 338, 53	1/2 Δ; 1.77	11
7.1.4-1a	CNG Triton VII, 522	O; 0.58	9
7.1.4-2a	G&M 142, 1686 = Rauch MBS 8, 144	O; 0.57	8
7.1.4-3a	Peus 386, 361	O; 0.61	8
Kamnaskires IV			
8.1.1-1Aa	CNG Triton VII, 523 = NFA XXV, 249 = SKA 3, 286 (obv. die linked to 8.1.1-1Ba)	4Δ; 16.08	27
8.1.1-1Ba	Peus 392, 4393 = Peus 386, 362 (obv. die linked to 8.1.1-1Aa)	4Δ; 15.47	26
8.1.2-1a	CNG 76, 934 (obv. die linked to 8.1.2-1b)	Δ; 3.78	17
8.1.2-1b	Peus 374. 127 = Peus 368, 333 (obv. die linked to 8.1.2-1a)	Δ; 3.70	15
8.1.2-2a	G&M 142, 1687	Δ; 3.84	15
8.1.2-3a	BMC p. 247, 1, pl. XXXVIII, 5	Δ; 3.93	15
8.1.2-3b	G&M 134, 1590 = G&M 130, 1312 = Peus 360, 256	Δ; 3.87	15
8.1.3-1a	CNG E-Auction 102, 61	O; 0.54	8
8.2.1-1a	Le Rider 1965, pl. LXXII, 13	4Δ; 15.94	26
8.2.2-1a	BMC p. 247, 2, pl. XXXVIII, 6	Δ; 3.56	17
8.2.2-1b	Peus 386, 363 (obv. die linked to 8.2.2-2a)	Δ; 3.53	16

APPENDIX 2 - SOURCES, WEIGHT, and SIZE

8.2.2-2a	Peus 386, 364 (obv. die linked to 8.2.2-1b)	Δ; 3.76	18
8.2.3-1a	Peus 368, 334	O; n/a[1]	8
8.2.3-1b	Rauch MBS 8, 145	O; 0.50	8
8.3.1-1a	CNG Triton VII, 524	4Δ; 15.36	28
8.3.2-1a	Peus 368, 335 (obv. die linked to 8.3.2-1b-d)	Δ; 3.79	17
8.3.2-1b	Peus 328, 285 (obv. die linked to 8.3.2-1a,c,d)	Δ; 3.68	17
8.3.2-1c	CNG 66, 833 (obv. die linked to 8.3.2-1a,b; obv. & rev. die linked to 8.3.2-1d)	Δ; 3.76	16
8.3.2-1d	Hansman 1990, pl. I, 1 (obv. die linked to 8.3.2-1a,b; obv. & rev. die linked to 8.3.2-1c)	Δ; n/a	n/a
8.3.2-2a	CNG Triton VII, 525 (obv. die linked to 8.3.2-2b,c)	Δ; 3.90	18
8.3.2-2b	Hansman 1990, pl. I, 2 (obv. die linked to 8.3.2-2a,c)	Δ; n/a	n/a
8.3.2-2c	Peus 386, 365 (obv. die linked to 8.3.2-2a,b)	Δ; 3.25	18
8.3.2-3a	Private collection (obv. die linked to 8.3.2-3b)	Δ; 4.07	17
8.3.2-3b	CNG E-Auction 122, 165 = CNG E-Auction 90, 68 = GM 55, 372 (obv. die linked to 8.3.2-3a)	Δ; 3.69	16
8.3.2-4a	G&M 130, 1313	Δ; 3.98	15
8.3.3-1a	Kovacs XIII, 89	1/2 Δ; 2.20	14
Kamnaskires V			
9.1.1-1a	Senior 1998, p. 18, 1	4Δ; 15.47	25
9.1.1-2a	Le Rider 1965, pl. LXXII, 18 = Ars Classica XII, 2531	4Δ; 15.07	25
9.1.1-3a	CNG 66, 834 = Kovacs X, 199	4Δ; 15.26	27
9.1.1-4a	Le Rider 1965, pl. LXXII, 17 = Ars Classica XII, 2532	4Δ; 15.70	26
9.1.1-5Aa	Baldwin's 44, 101 = New York Sale III, 201	4Δ; 11.10	23
9.1.1-5Ba	Baldwin's 43, 2064 = Baldwin's 40, 38	4Δ; 15.4	26
9.1.1-6a	CNG Triton VII, 521 = Kovacs XIII, 90	4Δ; 14.94	28
9.1.1-7a	Peus 368, 336	4Δ; 16.10	25
9.1.1-7b	CNG Triton VII, 526	4Δ; 15.05	28
9.1.1-7c	Le Rider 1965, pl. LXXII, 16 = De Morgan 14	4Δ; 14.98	27
9.1.1-7d	Le Rider 1965, pl. LXXII, 15 = Florange & Ciani, 17 Feb. 1925, 1458	4Δ; 15.85	28
9.1.1-7e	G&M 130, 1315	4Δ; 15.78	26
9.1.1-7f	Elsen FPL 202, 168	4Δ; 14.48	25
9.1.1-7g	G&M 134, 1591	4Δ; 14.38	25
9.1.1-7h	UBS 61, 4409	4Δ; 15.61	24
9.1.1-7i	G&M 130, 1316	4Δ; 14.73	27
9.1.2-1a	CNG 66, 835 (obv. die linked to 9.1.2-1b)	Δ; 3.68	15
9.1.2-1b	G&M 138, 1525 = CNG Triton VII, 527 (obv. die linked to 9.1.2-1a)	Δ; 3.24	17
9.1.2-2a	In commerce	Δ; 3.37	17
9.1.2-3a	Private collection	Δ; n/a	n/a
9.1.2-4Aa	Le Rider 1965, pl. LXXII, 14 = Ars Classica XII, 2534	Δ; 3.80	15
9.1.2-4Ba	Elsen 69, 302	Δ; 3.69	16
9.1.2-4Ca	Peus 386, 366	Δ; 3.27	15
9.1.2-5a	Peus 386, 368	Δ; 3.47	17
9.1.2-6Aa	Elsen 55, 347 = Peus 338, 57	Δ; 3.77	16
9.1.2-6Ab	Elsen FPL 121, 157	Δ; 3.85	n/a
9.1.2-6Ba	MuMD 16, 982 = Peus 338, 58	Δ; 3.66	13
9.1.3-1a	Peus 368, 337	1/2 Δ; 1.83	12
9.1.3-2a	G&M 118, 1545 = GM 101, 407	1/2 Δ; 1.82	11
9.1.3-3a	CNG Triton VII, 528	1/2 Δ; 1.62	12

[1] The listed weight in the Peus sale of 1.64 grams must be erroneous.

9.1.3-4a	G&M 138, 1526	1/2 Δ; 1.66	12
9.1.3-4b	Private collection	1/2 Δ; 1.48	11
9.1.4-1a	Kovacs XIII, 92	O; 0.61	8
9.1.4-2a	Alram 466 = BMC p. 249, 10, pl. XXXVIII, 13	O; 0.60	8
9.1.5-1a	Peus 368, 367	1/2 O; 0.42	8
9.2.1-1a	Peus 374, 129	Δ; 3.61	18

Uncertain Early Arsacid Kings

10.1.1-1a	Le Rider 1965, pl. LXXIII, 3	4Δ; 15.48	27
10.1.1-1b	Künker 94, 1508	4Δ; 15.01	26
10.1.2-1a	CNG E-Auction 90, 70 = Hirsch 166, 556	Δ; 3.36	15
10.1.2-1b	Elsen 71, 356	Δ; 3.82	13
10.1.2-1c	CNG 55, 773 (part of)	Δ; n/a	14
10.1.2-2a	Hansman 1990, pl. 1, 3	Δ; n/a	n/a
10.2.1-1a	CNG Triton VII, 529 (obv. die linked to 10.2.1-1a)	4Δ; 15.33	29
10.2.1-1b	G&M 108, 1390 (obv. die linked to 10.2.1-1b)	4Δ; 15.35	30
10.3.1-1Aa	Peus 333, 380	4Δ; 15.31	30
10.3.1-1Ab	Elsen 46, 342	4Δ; 15.32	29
10.3.1-1Ac	Private collection	4Δ; 14.28	29
10.3.1-1Ad	Peus 386, 369 = Peus 333, 379	4Δ; 14.14	30
10.3.1-1Ba	Elsen 41, 125	4Δ; 15.55	28
10.3.1-1Bb	CNG Triton VII, 531 = Vecchi 16, 304	4Δ; 15.42	29
10.3.1-1Ca	Elsen 28, 320 = G&M 130, 1320	4Δ; 14.93	29
10.3.1-1Cb	In commerce	4Δ; 15.7	28
10.3.1-1Da	CNG 57, 687	4Δ; 15.36	32
10.3.1-1Db	Peus 386, 371	4Δ; 15.44	29
10.3.1-2Aa	Private collection	4Δ; 15.41	27
10.3.1-2Ba	Private collection	4Δ; 14.76	22
10.3.2-1a	Elsen List 188, 139	Δ; 3.79	14
10.3.2-1b	Elsen List 225, 133	Δ; 3.62	16
10.3.2-1c	Private collection	Δ; 3.75	15
10.4.1-1a	Peus 386, 370	4Δ; 16.22	28
10.4.1-1b	Elsen 35, 192	4Δ; 13.69	28
10.4.1-2a	Elsen List 218, 263	4Δ; 14.76	26
10.4.2-1Aa	G&M 130, 1324	Δ; 3.54	19
10.4.2-1Ab	Private collection	Δ; 3.54	18
10.4.2-1Ba	Elsen 36, 236	Δ; 3.57	17
10.4.2-2Aa	CNG 75, 606 = CNG Triton VII, 530	Δ; 4.06	17
10.4.2-2Ab	Private collection	Δ; 3.5	n/a
10.4.2-2Ba	Private collection	Δ; 3.69	17
10.4.2-2Bb	G&M 130, 1325	Δ; 3.72	16
10.4.2-3a	Private collection	Δ; 3.50	18
10.4.2-3b	Le Rider 1965, pl. LXXIII, 10	Δ; n/a	18
10.4.2-4Aa	Private collection	Δ; 3.70	18
10.4.2-4Ab	Elsen 71, 357	Δ; 3.82	15
10.4.2-4Ac	In commerce	Δ; 3.2	16
10.4.2-4Ad	In commerce	Δ; 3.5	15
10.4.2-4Ae	In commerce	Δ; 3.7	16
10.4.2-4Ba	Augé 1979, pl. 4, 20	Δ; 4.73	17

Orodes I

11.1.1-1a	CNG 60, 1041	4Δ; 15.74	27
11.1.1-1b	CNG 63, 884	4Δ; 15.40	27

APPENDIX 2 - SOURCES, WEIGHT, and SIZE

11.1.1-1c	CNG Triton VII, 532	4Δ; 15.54	27
11.1.1-1d	Private collection	4Δ; 15.57	n/a
11.1.1-2a	GM 92, 288 (obv. die linked to 11.1.1-1Bb)	4Δ; 15.27	29
11.1.1-2b	Peus 386, 372 (obv. die linked to 11.1.1-1Ba)	4Δ; 15.24	29
11.2.1-1a	Private collection	4Δ; 13.34	n/a
11.2.1-1b	Private collection	4Δ; 13.50	n/a
11.2.1-2a	Alram NB3	4Δ; 15.05	30
Kamnaskires-Orodes			
12.1.1-1Aa	Album 180, 150	4Δ; 14.63	30
12.1.1-1Ab	CNG Triton VII, 534	4Δ; 15.16	27
12.1.1-1Ba	Alram 479 = Florange & Ciani, 17 Feb. 1925, 1466	4Δ; n/a	28
12.1.1-1Ca	Augé 1979, pl. 16, 2371	4Δ; 15.18	28
12.1.1-2a	Le Rider 1965, pl. LXXIII, 8 (obv. die linked to 12.2.1-1b)	4Δ; n/a	28
12.1.1-2b	Augé 1979, pl. 15, 2061 (obv. die linked to 12.2.1-1a)	4Δ; 14.09	26
12.1.1-3Aa	Augé 1979, pl. 14, 2045	4Δ; 15.01	28
12.1.1-3Ba	Alram 480 = Allotte de la Füye, *RN* 1919, pl. 1, 10	4Δ; n/a	28
12.1.1-3Ca	Le Rider 1965, pl. LXXIII, 7	4Δ; n/a	27
12.1.1-3Da	Augé 1979, pl. 14, 2052 (obv. die linked to 12.1.1-3b-c)	4Δ; 15.06	28
12.1.1-3Db	Augé 1979, pl. 14, 2054 (obv. die linked to 12.1.1-3a and c)	4Δ; 15.l4	28
12.1.1-3Dc	G&M 130, 1330 (obv. die linked to 12.1.1-3a-b)	4Δ; 14.35	28
12.1.1-3Ea	Augé 1979, pl. 15, 2057	4Δ; 14.89	27
12.1.1-3Fa	CNG Triton VII, 535	4Δ; 15.09	27
12.2.1-1Aa	Augé 1979, pl. 16, 2391 (obv. die linked to 12.5.1-1b)	Δ; 3.53	14
12.2.1-1Ab	Augé 1979, pl. 16, 2392 (obv. die linked to 12.5.1-1a)	Δ; 372	14
12.2.1-1Ba	Augé 1979, pl. 16, 2373	Δ; 3.76	15
12.2.1-1Bb	Augé 1979, pl. 16, 2375	Δ; 3.84	15
12.2.1-1Ca	Augé 1979, pl. 16, 2374	Δ; 3.83	14
12.2.1-1Cb	Augé 1979, pl. 16, 2381	Δ; 4.25	15
12.2.1-1Cc	Alram 482 = Le Rider 1965, pl. LXXIII, 24	Δ; n/a	14
12.2.1-1Da	Private collection	Δ; 3.72	16
12.2.1-1Db	Private collection	Δ; 3.40	15
12.2.1-1Ea	Private collection	Δ; 3.27	16
12.2.1-2Aa	Augé 1979, pl. 15, 2062	Δ; 3.57	15
12.2.1-2Ab	Augé 1979, pl. 15, 2065	Δ; 3.74	15
12.2.1-2Ba	Augé 1979, pl. 15, 2067	Δ; 3.51	14
12.2.1-2Bb	Augé 1979, pl. 15, 2068	Δ; 3.51	15
12.3.1-1Aa	Elsen List 192, 109	Δ; 3.72	15
12.3.1-1Ab	Augé 1979, pl. 16, 2393	Δ; 3.64	16
12.3.1-1Ac	Augé 1979, pl. 16, 2406	Δ; 3.82	16
12.3.1-1Ba	Private collection	Δ; 3.84	15
12.3.1-1Bb	Augé 1979, pl. 16, 2417	Δ; 3.47	16
12.3.1-1Bc	Elsen List 188, 141	Δ; 3.84	15
12.3.1-1Bd	Augé 1979, pl. 17, 2427	Δ; 3.50	15
12.3.1-1Be	Private collection	Δ; 3.69	15
12.3.1-1Bf	Augé 1979, pl. 17, 2448	Δ; 3.76	15
12.3.1-2A1a	Augé 1979, pl. 15, 2074	Δ; 3.70	15
12.3.1-2A1b	Augé 1979, pl. 15, 2184	Δ; 3.61	17
12.3.1-2A1c	Private collection	Δ; 3.55	15
12.3.1-2A1d	Private collection	Δ; 3.48	14
12.3.1-2A1e	Augé 1979, pl. 15, 2084	Δ; 3.30	16
12.3.1-2A2a	Private collection	Δ; 3.89	15

12.3.1-2A2b	Private collection	Δ; 3.73	15
12.3.1-2A2c	Augé 1979, pl. 15, 2104	Δ; 3.55	15
12.3.1-2A2d	Augé 1979, pl. 15, 2128	Δ; 4.00	15
12.3.1-2A2e	Private collection	Δ; 3.90	16
12.3.1-2A2f	Augé 1979, pl. 15, 2168	Δ; 3.41	15
12.3.1-2A2g	Augé 1979, pl. 16, 2281	Δ; 3.68	14
12.3.1-2B1a	Elsen List 200, 79	Δ; 3.47	15
12.3.1-2B1b	Augé 1979, pl. 16, 2320	Δ; 3.19	14
12.3.1-2B1c	Augé 1979, pl. 16, 2298	Δ; 4.33	15
12.3.1-2B1d	Private collection	Δ; 3.75	15
12.3.1-2B1e	Private collection	Δ; 3.62	15
12.3.1-2B1f	Augé 1979, pl. 16, 2305	Δ; 3.76	15
12.3.1-2B1g	Augé 1979, pl. 16, 2356	Δ; 3.69	15
12.3.1-2B2a	Augé 1979, pl. 16, 2322	Δ; 3.58	15
12.3.1-2B2b	Private collection	Δ; 3.26	16
12.3.1-2B2c	Augé 1979, pl. 16, 2334	Δ; 3.50	15
12.3.1-2B2d	Augé 1979, pl. 16, 2361	Δ; 3.86	15
12.3.1-2B2e	Augé 1979, pl. 16, 2363	Δ; 3.99	17
12.4.1-1a	Alram 486 = BMC p. cxcii, pl. 53, 16 = De Morgan 51 (unillustrated).	Δ; n/a	15
Orodes II			
13.1.1-1a	Elsen 63, 1273Δ; 3.73	Δ; 3.73	15
13.1.1-1b	Augé 1979, pl. 14, 2000	Δ; 3.40	15
13.1.1-1c	Augé 1979, pl. 14, 2001	Δ; 2.55	15
13.1.1-2a	Private collection	Δ; 3.65	16
13.1.1-2b	Private collection	Δ; 3.55	16
13.1.1-2c	Augé 1979, pl. 14, 2024	Δ; 3.35	14
13.1.1-2d	Augé 1979, pl. 14, 2034	Δ; 3.26	15
13.1.1-2e	Augé 1979, pl. 14, 2035	Δ; 3.26	17
13.1.1-2f	Augé 1979, pl. 14, 2038	Δ; 3.22	15
13.1.1-2g	Augé 1979, pl. 14, 2044	Δ; 4.23	15
13.1.1-2h	Alram 485 = Le Rider 1965, pl. LXXIII, 23	Δ; n/a	17
13.2.1-1Aa	Augé 1979, pl. 11, 1497	Δ; 3.57	15
13.2.1-1Ba	Augé 1979, pl. 11, 1504	Δ; 3.81	14
13.2.1-1Bb	Augé 1979, pl. 14, 1922	Δ; 3.56	15
13.2.1-2Aa	Augé 1979, pl. 11, 1509	Δ; 3.71	15
13.2.1-2Ab	Augé 1979, pl. 11, 1512	Δ; 4.16	16
13.2.1-2Ac	Augé 1979, pl. 11, 1513	Δ; 3.00	15
13.2.1-2Ad	Augé 1979, pl. 11, 1519	Δ; 3.64	14
13.2.1-2Ba	Private collection	Δ; 3.73	15
13.2.1-2Bb	Private collection	Δ; 3.39	15
13.2.1-2Bc	Augé 1979, pl. 11, 1522	Δ; 4.10	17
13.2.1-2Bd	Augé 1979, pl. 11, 1534	Δ; 3.57	17
13.2.1-2Be	Augé 1979, pl. 11, 1569	Δ; 3.63	15
13.2.1-2Bf	In commerce	Δ; 3.0	15
13.2.1-2Bg	Augé 1979, pl. 14, 1923	Δ; 3.17	15
13.2.1-2Bh	Augé 1979, pl. 14, 1925	Δ; 3.70	15
13.2.1-2Bi	Private collection	Δ; 3.82	15
13.2.1-2Bj	Private collection	Δ; 3.74	14
13.2.1-2Bk	Augé 1979, pl. 11, 1544	Δ; 3.67	14
13.2.1-2Ca	Private collection	Δ; 3.77	14

13.2.1-2Cb	Augé 1979, pl. 11, 1584	Δ; 3.40	14
13.2.1-2Cc	Augé 1979, pl. 11, 1606	Δ; 3.99	14
13.2.1-2Cd	Augé 1979, pl. 11, 1599	Δ; 3.55	15
13.2.1-2Ce	Augé 1979, pl. 11, 1586	Δ; 3.56	14
13.3.1-1a	Augé 1979, pl. 12, 1891	4Δ; 15.09	28
13.3.1-2a	Augé 1979, pl. 12, 2632	4Δ; 14.39	27
13.3.1-2b	CNG Triton VI, 1580 (part of)	4Δ; 16.06	28
13.3.1-3Aa	Augé 1979, pl. 13, 1903	4Δ; 15.40	27
13.3.1-3Ba	Augé 1979, pl. 13, 1912	4Δ; 14.84	26
13.3.1-3Ca	Augé 1979, pl. 13, 1920	4Δ; 14.70	29
13.3.1-4a	Augé 1979, pl. 12, 1899	4Δ; 15.09	28
13.3.2-1Aa	Private collection	Δ; 3.74	15
13.3.2-1Ab	Private collection	Δ; 3.71	15
13.3.2-1Ac	Private collection	Δ; 3.63	14
13.3.2-1Ad	Augé 1979, pl. 11, 1634	Δ; 3.96	15
13.3.2-1Ae	Augé 1979, pl. 11, 1641	Δ; 3.61	15
13.3.2-1Ba	Augé 1979, pl. 14, 1927	Δ; 3.02	16
13.3.2-1Bb	Augé 1979, pl. 14, 1929	Δ; 3.53	15
13.3.2-2Aa	Private collection	Δ; 3.60	15
13.3.2-2Ab	Private collection	Δ; 3.40	16
13.3.2-2Ac	Augé 1979, pl. 11, 1659	Δ; 3.74	15
13.3.2-2Ad	Augé 1979, pl. 11, 1666	Δ; 3.20	16
13.3.2-2Ae	Augé 1979, pl. 11, 1759	Δ; 3.45	15
13.3.2-2Af	Augé 1979, pl. 11, 1704	Δ; 3.84	16
13.3.2-2Ag	Private collection	Δ; 3.54	16
13.3.2-2Ba	Private collection	Δ; 3.43	14
13.3.2-2Bb	Augé 1979, pl. 14, 1959	Δ; 3.51	15
13.3.2-2Bc	Augé 1979, pl. 14, 1964	Δ; 3.57	16
1513.3.2-2Bd	Augé 1979, pl. 14, 1988	Δ; 3.60	15
13.3.2-2Be	Augé 1979, pl. 14, 1998	Δ; 3.99	14
13.3.2-2Ca	Private collection	Δ; 3.43	14
Phraates			
14.1.1-1Aa	Private collection	Δ; 3.38	14
14.1.1-1Ab	Augé 1979, pl. 9, 1195	Δ; 3.99	15
14.1.1-1Ac	Augé 1979, pl. 9, 1196	Δ; 4.10	14
14.1.1-1Ba	Private collection	Δ; 3.26	15
14.1.1-1Bb	Augé 1979, pl. 9, 1179	Δ; 3.35	15
14.1.1-1Bc	Augé 1979, pl. 9, 1185	Δ; 3.76	14
14.1.1-1Ca	Private collection	Δ; 3.38	15
14.1.1-1Cb	Elsen 63, 1272	Δ; 3.73	15
14.1.1-2Aa	Private collection	Δ; 2.76	15
14.1.1-2Ab	Augé 1979, pl. 9, 1206	Δ; 3.58	14
14.1.1-2Ba	Augé 1979, pl. 9, 1187	Δ; 3.39	14
14.1.1-2Ca	Augé 1979, pl. 9, 1227	Δ; 3.60	15
14.1.1-2Cb	Augé 1979, pl. 9, 1232	Δ; 3.92	16
14.2.1-1a	Augé 1979, pl. 10, 1275	Δ; 3.10	14
14.2.1-2Aa	Private collection	Δ; 2.96	14
14.2.1-2Ab	Private collection	Δ; 3.28	14
14.2.1-2Ac	Elsen 55, 349	Δ; 3.24	14
14.2.1-2Ad	Augé 1979, pl. 10, 1288	Δ; 3.16	15
14.2.1-2Ae	Augé 1979, pl. 10, 1283	Δ; 3.10	14

14.2.1-2Af	Augé 1979, pl. 10, 1347	Δ; 3.68	15
14.2.1-2Ag	Augé 1979, pl. 10, 1296	Δ; 2.45	14
14.2.1-2Ah	Augé 1979, pl. 10, 1363	Δ; 2.87	14
14.2.1-2Ai	Augé 1979, pl. 9, 1264	Δ; 2.48	15
14.2.1-2Ba	Private collection	Δ; 2.89	14
14.2.1-2Ca	Augé 1979, pl. 10, 1277	Δ; 2.46	16
14.2.1-3a	Private collection	Δ; 3.40	15
14.2.1-4Aa	Private collection	Δ; 3.60	16
14.2.1-4Ab	Private collection	Δ; 3.37	14
14.2.1-4Ac	Augé 1979, pl. 9, 1261	Δ; 3.40	16
14.2.1-4Ad	Le Rider 1965, pl. LXXIV, 2	Δ; n/a	15
14.2.1-4Ba	Augé 1979, pl. 10, 1438	Δ; 3.55	15
14.2.1-5a	Private collection	Δ; 3.27	15
14.2.1-5b	Augé 1979, pl. 10, 1266	Δ; 2.21	15
14.3.1-1a	Augé 1979, pl. 10, 1459	Δ; 2.89	14
14.3.1-1b	Augé 1979, pl. 10, 1462	Δ; 3.75	14
14.3.1-1c	Private collection	Δ; 2.28	13
14.3.1-2a	Augé 1979, pl. 10, 1454	Δ; 2.96	14
14.4.1-1Aa	Private collection	Δ; 2.96	14
14.4.1-1Ab	Le Rider 1965, pl. LXIV, 3	Δ; n/a	15
14.4.1-1Ac	Augé 1979, pl. 9, 1241	Δ; 3.26	14
14.4.1-1Ad	Augé 1979, pl. 9, 1247	Δ; 3.45	15
14.4.1-1Ae	Augé 1979, pl. 10, 1393	Δ; 3.80	15
14.4.1-1Ba	Augé 1979, pl. 10, 1385	Δ; 2.51	15
14.4.1-1Ca	Augé 1979, pl. 10, 1434	Δ; 2.77	15
14.4.1-1Cb	Augé 1979, pl. 10, 1435	Δ; 3.80	15
14.4.1-1Cc	In commerce	Δ; n/a	n/a
14.4.1-1Cd	Private collection	Δ; 3.02	14
14.4.1-2a	Augé 1979, pl. 10, 1432	Δ; 3.19	13
14.4.1-2b	Augé 1979, pl. 10, 1433	Δ; 3.39	14
14.4.1-3a	Augé 1979, pl. 9, 1257	Δ; 3.97	15
14.5.1-1a	Augé 1979, pl. 10, 1467	Δ; 2.59	14
14.5.1-1b	Augé 1979, pl. 10, 1473	Δ; 3.40	15
14.5.1-1c	Augé 1979, pl. 10, 1491	Δ; 3.33	14
14.5.1-1d	Augé 1979, pl. 10, 1492	Δ; 3.40	15
14.5.1-2a	Augé 1979, pl. 10, 1477	Δ; 3.49	15
14.5.1-2b	Private collection	Δ; 3.11	15
14.6.1-1a	Augé 1979, pl. 8, 807	Δ; 3.42	15
14.6.1-2a	Private collection	Δ; 3.41	15
14.6.1-2b	Augé 1979, pl. 8, 860	Δ; 3.56	15
14.6.1-3a	Private collection	Δ; 3.69	15
14.6.1-3b	Private collection	Δ; 3.74	15
14.6.1-3c	Private collection	Δ; 3.82	15
14.7.1-1Aa	Alram 472 = Augé 1979, pl. 8, 806	4Δ; n/a	32
14.7.1-1Ba	Album 202, 230	4Δ; 14.45	30
14.7.1-2a	Alram 471 = Le Rider 1965, pl. LXXIII, 9	4Δ; 14.64	29
14.7.2-1a	Private collection	Δ; 3.94	17
14.7.2-1b	Private collection	Δ; 3.46	14
14.7.2-1c	Augé 1979, pl. 9, 1035	Δ; 3.71	15
14.7.2-1d	Augé 1979, pl. 9, 1064	Δ; 3.43	15
14.7.2-2Aa	Elsen 71, 359	Δ; 3.36	15

APPENDIX 2 - SOURCES, WEIGHT, and SIZE

14.7.2-2Ab	Augé 1979, pl. 8, 980	Δ; 3.55	14
14.7.2-2Ac	Augé 1979, pl. 8, 983	Δ; 3.92	15
14.7.2-2Ba	Elsen 69, 308	Δ; 3.42	15
14.7.2-2Bb	Augé 1979, pl. 8, 972	Δ; 3.50	15
14.7.2-3a	Augé 1979, pl. 8, 958	Δ; 3.42	15
14.7.2-3b	Augé 1979, pl. 8, 963	Δ; 3.73	15
14.7.2-3c	Augé 1979, pl. 8, 964	Δ; 3.76	15
14.7.2-3d	Augé 1979, pl. 8, 967	Δ; 3.85	15
14.8.1-1a	Peus 374, 130	4Δ; 14.94	28
14.8.1-1b	Peus 388, 275	4Δ; 16.45	29
Osroes			
15.1.1-1a	Le Rider 1965, pl. LXXIII, 31	Δ; 3.60	19
15.2.1-1a	Le Rider 1965, pl. LXXIII, 34	Δ; 3.60	16
15.3.1-1a	Le Rider 1965, pl. LXXIII, 36	O; 0.64	9
Orodes III			
16.1.1-1a	Private collection	Δ; 3.50	14
16.1.1-1b	Private collection	Δ; 3.25	14
16.1.1-1c	Private collection	Δ; 3.01	16
16.1.1-1d	Elsen 71, 358	Δ; 3.40	14
16.1.1-1e	Private collection	Δ; 3.84	14
16.1.1-2a	Private collection	Δ; 2.88	14
16.1.1-2b	Private collection	Δ; 2.95	14
16.1.1-3Aa	Private collection	Δ; 3.98	13
16.1.1-3Ab	Private collection	Δ; 3.15	15
16.1.1-3Ac	Private collection	Δ; 2.71	16
16.1.1-3Ad	Private collection	Δ; n/a	15
16.1.1-3Ba	Private collection	Δ; 2.84	15
16.2.1-1a	Private collection	Δ; 2.71	15
16.2.1-1b	Elsen 69, 305	Δ; 3.10	15
16.2.1-1c	Augé 1979, pl. 6, 334	Δ; 3.31	14
16.2.1-2Aa	Private collection	Δ; 3.20	16
16.2.1-2Ab	Augé 1979, pl. 6, 349	Δ; 2.88	13
16.2.1-2Ac	In commerce	Δ; 3.5	15
16.2.1-2Ad	In commerce	Δ; 3.0	13
16.2.1-2Ba	Private collection	Δ; 2.58	14
16.2.1-2Bb	Elsen 69, 306	Δ; 2.85	14
16.2.1-2Ca	Private collection	Δ; 3.38	14
16.2.1-2Cb	Augé 1979, pl. 6, 373	Δ; 2.79	14
16.2.1-3a	Augé 1979, pl. 6, 347	Δ; 3.42	14
16.2.1-4a	Augé 1979, pl. 6, 341	Δ; 2.84	14
16.2.1-4b	Augé 1979, pl. 6, 342	Δ; 2.84	14
16.3.1-1a	Augé 1979, pl. 5, 70 (obv. die linked to 16.4.1-1a)	4Δ; 14.16	30
16.3.1-2a	Augé 1979, pl. 5, 75 (obv. die linked to 16.4.1-2a)	4Δ; 13.91	27
16.3.2-1Aa	Private collection	Δ; 3.55	15
16.3.2-1Ab	Private collection	Δ; 3.23	15
16.3.2-1Ac	Private collection	Δ; 2.97	15
16.3.2-1Ad	Private collection	Δ; 3.38	14
16.3.2-1Ba	Augé 1979, pl. 7, 502	Δ; 3.26	15
16.3.2-1Ca	Augé 1979, pl. 7, 515	Δ; 3.92	15
16.3.2-1Da	Augé 1979, pl. 7, 526	Δ; 3.80	15
16.3.2-1Ea	Augé 1979, pl. 7, 520	Δ; 3.23	15

16.3.2-2Aa	Private collection	Δ; 3.47	15
16.3.2-2Ab	Private collection	Δ; 3.55	15
16.3.2-2Ac	Elsen List 212, 158	Δ; 3.50	15
16.3.2-2Ba	Augé 1979, pl. 7, 518	Δ; 2.63	15
16.3.2-2Bb	Augé 1979, pl. 7, 519	Δ; 2.95	15
16.3.2-2Ca	Augé 1979, pl. 7, 522	Δ; 3.44	15
16.4.1-1a	Le Rider 1965, pl. LXXIII, 5 (obv. die linked to 16.3.1-1a)	4Δ; 14.40	30
16.4.1-2a	CNG Triton VII, 533 (obv. die linked to 16.3.1-2a)	4Δ; 14.68	27
16.4.2-1Aa	Private collection	Δ; 3.72	15
16.4.2-1Ab	Private collection	Δ; 3.97	16
16.4.2-1Ac	Augé 1979, pl. 7, 721	Δ; 3.23	15
16.4.2-1Ba	Augé 1979, pl. 7, 683	Δ; 2.73	13
16.4.2-1Bb	Augé 1979, pl. 7, 688	Δ; 2.70	17
16.4.2-1Bc	Augé 1979, pl. 7, 692	Δ; 3.50	15
16.4.2-1Bd	Augé 1979, pl. 7, 693	Δ; 3.62	16
16.4.2-2a	Private collection	Δ; 2.53	15
16.4.2-2b	Private collection	Δ; 3.71	14
Orodes IV			
17.1.1-1a	Private collection	Δ; 3.35	14
17.1.1-1b	Elsen 63, 1274	Δ; 2.70	13
17.1.1-1c	Private collection	Δ; 3.71	14
17.1.1-1d	Private collection	Δ; 3.69	15
17.1.1-1e	In commerce	Δ; n/a	n/a
17.1.1-2a	Elsen 62, 419	Δ; 2.60	14
17.1.1-2b	Elsen 69, 310	Δ; 2.79	13
17.1.1-2c	Private collection	Δ; 2.41	14
17.2.1-1a	Private collection	Δ; 3.11	14
17.2.1-1b	Private collection	Δ; 3.22	14
17.2.1-1c	Private collection	Δ; 3.08	15
17.2.1-1d	In commerce	Δ; 2.5	13
17.2.1-2a	Le Rider 1965, pl. LXXIV, 6	Δ; n/a	14
17.3.1-1a	Elsen 61, 186 (part of)	Δ; n/a	13
17.3.1-2Aa	CNG 63, 885	Δ; 3.50	15
17.3.1-2Ab	In commerce	Δ; n/a	n/a
17.3.1-2Ba	Private collection	Δ; 2.86	13
17.3.1-2Bb	In commerce	Δ; n/a	n/a
Orodes V			
18.1.1-1Aa	Private collection	Δ; 2.65	16
18.1.1-1Ab	Augé 1979, pl. 17, 2460	Δ; 2.50	14
18.1.1-1Ac	Private collection	Δ; 2.84	14
18.1.1-1Ba	Private collection	Δ; 3.29	16
18.1.1-2Aa	Private collection	Δ; 2.15	12
18.1.1-2Ab	Private collection	Δ; 3.18	15
18.1.1-2Ac	Private collection	Δ; 2.34	12
18.1.1-2Ad	Private collection	Δ; 2.09	13
18.1.1-2Ba	Private collection	Δ; n/a	n/a
18.1.1-2Bb	Private collection	Δ; 2.2	n/a
18.1.1-2Bc	Le Rider 1965, pl. LXXIV, 4	Δ; n/a	14
18.1.1-2Bd	Private collection	Δ; 3.16	13
18.1.1-2Ca	In commerce	Δ; n/a	n/a

APPENDIX 2 - SOURCES, WEIGHT, and SIZE

Prince A			
19.1.1-1Aa	Private collection	Δ; 2.60	13
19.1.1-1Ab	Private collection	Δ; 2.13	15
19.1.1-1Ac	Private collection	Δ; 1.99	12
19.1.1-1Ad	Elsen 62, 420	Δ; 1.72	11
19.1.1-1Ae	Le Rider 1965, pl. LXXIV, 7	Δ; n/a	14
19.1.1-1Af	Le Rider 1965, pl. LXXIV, 8	Δ; n/a	13
19.1.1-1Ag	In commerce	Δ; n/a	n/a
19.1.1-1Ah	Private collection	Δ; 2.12	13
19.1.1-1Ai	Private collection	Δ; 2.78	13
19.1.1-1Ba	Private collection	Δ; 3.07	14
19.1.1-1Bb	Private collection	Δ; 1.90	13
19.1.1-1Bc	Elsen 69, 313	Δ; 1.66	12
19.1.1-1Bd	Elsen 71, 363	Δ; 2.25	12
19.1.1-1Be	Private collection	Δ; 1.58	12
19.1.1-1Bf	Private collection	Δ; 1.77	12
19.1.1-2a	Private collection	Δ; 2.29	12
Prince B			
20.1.1-1Aa	Elsen 69, 311	Δ; 2.92	14
20.1.1-1Ab	Private collection	Δ; 2.95	14
20.1.1-1Ba	Augé 1979, pl. 17, 2465	Δ; 2.78	14
20.1.1-1Bb	Augé 1979, pl. 17, 2466	Δ; 3.10	13
20.1.1-2a	Private collection	Δ; 2.40	8
20.1.2-1a	Augé 1979, pl. 17, 2700	U; 1.45	12
Unidentified King			
21.1.1-1a	Le Rider 1965, pl. LXXIV, 11	U; n/a	9
21.1.1-1b	Augé 1979, pl. 17, 2705	U; 1.36	10
21.1.1-2a	Augé 1979, pl. 17, 2702	U; 1.64	11
21.1.2-1a	Augé 1979, pl. 17, 2711	U; 2.27	11

Bibliography

Allotte de la Füye, François Maurice. "Monnaies de l'Elymaide." In *Mémoires de la Délégation en perse*. Vol. 8. Chartres: 1905.

Alram, Michael. *Nomina Propria Iranica in Nvmmis*. Vol. 4 of *Iranisches Personennamenbuch*. Vienna: Verlag der Östereichischen Akademie der Wissenschaften, 1986.

Assar, G.R.F. "Recent Studies in Parthian History." Parts 1-3. *The Celator* 14, no. 12 (December 2000): 6-22; 15, no. 1 (January 2001): 17-27, 41; 15, no. 2 (February 2001): 17-22.

———. *History and Coinage of Elymais during 150/149 – 122/121*. Unpublished. 2005.

———. "A Revised Parthian Chronology of the Period 91-55 BC." In *Parthica*. Vol. 8. Pisa: Istituti editoriali e poligrafici internazionali, 2006.

Augé, C, et al. *Terrasses sacrées de Bard-è Néchandeh et Masjid-i Solaiman. Les trouvailles monétaires*, Mémoires de la Delégation Archéologique en Iran, Tome XLVI, Paris: Librairie Orientaliste Paul Geuthner, 1979.

Bell, Benjamin R. "New Inscription Alters Elymais Type Chronology." In *The Celator* 16, no. 4 (April 2002): 38-9, 50.

———. "A New Model for Elymaean Royal Chronology." In *The Celator* 16, no. 5 (May 2002): 34-9, 50, 59.

Dabrowa, Edward. "Zeugnisse zur Geschichte der Parthischen Susiane und Elymais." In *Das Partherreich und seine Zeugnisse*. Stuttgart: Franz Steiner Verlag, 1998.

Dobbins, Ed. "Hoard evidence aids attribution and chronology of Arsacid bronze drachms of Elymais." In *The Celator* 6, No. 8 (August 1992): 42-5.

Fischer, Thomas. "Βασιλεως Καμνισκ(ε)ιρου." In *Chiron* 1 (1971): 169-175.

Ghirshman, R. *Terrasses sacré de Bard-é Néchandeh te Mashid-i Soleiman*. Vol. 45 of *Memoires de la Délégation Archéologique en Iran*. Paris: 1976.

Green, Peter. *Alexander of Macedon, 336-323: A Historical Biography*. London: Pelican, 1974. Reprint, Berkeley: University of California Press, 1991.

Hansman, John. "The Great Gods of Elymais." In Vol. 1 of *Papers in Honour of Professor Mary Boyce*. Acta Iranica, 2d ser., vol. 24. Leuven: Peeters, 1985.

———. "Coins and Mints of Ancient Elymais." In *Iran*. Vol. 28. London: British Academy, 1990.

———. "Elymais." In *Encyclopaedia Iranica*. Internet database. Center for Iranian Studies, Columbia University, New York. http://www.iranica.com/.

Hill, George Francis. *Catalogue of the Greek coins of Arabia, Mesopotamia, and Persia*. Vol. 28 of *A Catalogue of Greek Coins in the British Museum*. London: Printed by order of the Trustees, 1922.

Le Rider, Georges. *Suse sous les Seleucides et les Parthes*. Vol. 38 of *Mission Archéologique en Iran*. Paris: Libraire Paul Geuthner, 1965.

———. "Monnaies grecques récemment acquises par le cabinet de Paris." In *Revue Numismatique*, 6th ser., vol. 11 (1969): 7-27.

———. "Deu nouveaux tetradrachmes frappés a Suse." In *Revue Numismatique*, 6th ser., vol. 20 (1978): 33-7.

Michener, Michael. *Oriental Coins and their Values. The Ancient and Classical World.* London: Hawkins Publications, 1978.

De Morgan, Jacques. *Ancient Persian Numismatics: Elymais.* Translated by D.G. Churchill. Paris, 1930. Reprint, New York: Attic Books, 1976.

Petrowicz, Alexander von. *Arsaciden Münzen.* Vienna: 1904. Reprint, Graz: 1968.

Potts, Daniel T. *The Archaeology of Elam.* Cambridge: Cambridge University Press, 1999.

Sachs, A.J., and Hermann Hunger. *Diaries from 164 B.C. to 61 B.C.* Vol. 3 of *Astronomical Diaries and Related texts from Babylonia.* Vienna: Verlag der Österreichischen Akademie, 1996

Sellwood, David. *An Intoduction to the Coinage of Parthia.* 2nd ed. London: Spink & Son Ltd., 1980.

Senior, Robert C. "Notes on a few ancient coins." In *Oriental Numismatic Society Newsletter* 155 (1998): 18.

Shore, Fred B. *Parthian Coins and History: Ten dragons against Rome.* Quarryville, PA: Classical Numismatic Group, 1993.

Vardanian, R. "Elimaidskie monety: k khronologicheskoæi sistematizaëtisii bronzorykh emissiæi II v.n.e." [Elymaean coins: a chronological systemisation of bronze emissions in the second century A.D.] In *Vestnik Drevnej Istorii,* 176/1 (1986): 99-117.